About this Learning Guide

Shmoop Will Make You a Better Lover*
*of Literature, History, Poetry, Life...

Our lively learning guides are written by experts and educators who want to show your brain a good time. Shmoop writers come primarily from Ph.D. programs at top universities, including Stanford, Harvard, and UC Berkeley.

Want more Shmoop? We cover literature, poetry, bestsellers, music, US history, civics, biographies (and the list keeps growing). Drop by our website to see the latest.

www.shmoop.com

©2010 Shmoop University, Inc. All Rights Reserved.
Talk to the Labradoodle... She's in Charge.

Table of Contents

Introduction

In a Nutshell

Frankenstein is the story of Victor Frankenstein, a brilliant Swiss scientist who discovers the secret of bringing inanimate things to life, eventually creating a human-like monster which proceeds to ruin his life. Most impressive is that Mary Shelley wrote this when she was nineteen. We don't know about you, but we certainly weren't writing earth-shattering, Halloween-costume-generating, horror-movie-spawning literature before we turned twenty. The novel made an impact at the time because of the oh-so-recent Industrial Revolution (1820s-ish). People were scared about these new "science" fields that were apparently capable of ungodly horrors. *Frankenstein*, like any good, famous novel, remarks on the times and reflects the emotions of society at large, namely their fears of science and technology.

Why Should I Care?

Frankenstein couldn't possibly have anything to do with our world. We mean, aside from the fact that it's partially responsible for the genre of science fiction, it has seared our collective cultural imagination, it has inspired countless monster movies (Tim Burton's among them), Halloween costumes, parodies, TV characters (think shows like *Scooby Doo* and *The Munsters*), and achieved all-around legend status, seriously, it's like, *antiquated*.

It's not as though we in the modern world could possibly relate to a terrifying fear of scientific advancement. The entire emerging field of genetics hasn't created any controversy at all. It's not as though the President had an entire team of professionals debate the topic and publish a report (that would be *Human Cloning and Human Dignity: The Report of the President's Council on Bioethics*) condemning the entire practice and prohibiting many potential venues for further work. It's not as though stem cell research is a hot topic these days. Right?

The fact is, if Dolly the sheep is our version of Victor's late-night lab putzing, then *Gattaca* and *X-Men* are our versions of *Frankenstein*: our collective fears manifested in fantastical, narrative tales. Yes, we did just compare Dolly to Frankenstein's monster. Just picture the loveable sheep chasing after you with a machete in hand (hoof?), and you'll get there.

Which brings us to the whole appearances thing. *Star*, *People*, E!, those speculations about Brad and Angelina's offspring – we are obsessed with how people look. Maybe we aren't so different from Victor after all.

In short, you are welcome to hail *Frankenstein* as irrelevant – as long as you have 1) never heard of bioethics, 2) never seen an actor with more good looks than talent, and 3) never turned down that sweet-but-homely member of the opposite sex who would have done anything to go to prom with you.

Summary

Book Summary

The story begins with Captain Robert Walton sailing to the North Pole in the 18th century. Unfortunately, the boat gets stuck in impassible ice hundreds of miles from land. With nothing else to do, he writes letters to his sister back in England. He's pretty boring, as far as we can tell. He tells his sister that he wants a male friend to keep him company.

Soon, Walton's despair is interrupted by the sight of – a man! On the ice! Riding a dog-sled! The man boards the ship, and it seems as if Walton's wish for a friend has come true. But this new guy Victor? Kind of nuts.

Victor recounts his life story to Walton as he rests aboard the ship. Victor started out like any normal kid in Geneva. His parents adopted a girl named Elizabeth for him to marry when he was older. (That won't be weird.) In the normal progression of things, Victor gets older and goes off to college to study natural philosophy and chemistry. He also renews his interest in alchemy. In about two years (which, by the way, is one third of a Ph.D. in the U.S.), he figures out how to bring a body made of human corpse pieces to life. Afterwards, he is horrified by his own creation (no…really?) and falls ill. Lucky for him, his friend, Henry, nurses him back to health.

Back in Geneva, Victor's younger brother, William, is murdered. The Frankenstein family servant, Justine, is accused of killing him. Victor magically intuits that it is the monster that killed William and that Justine is innocent. Thinking no one would believe the "my monster did it" excuse, Victor is afraid to even propose his theory. Even when poor Justine is executed.

Victor, in grief, goes on a trip to the Swiss Alps for some much-needed rest and relaxation. All too conveniently, he runs into the monster, who confesses to the crime. The monster tells a sad and moving story about how he has been alienated from the world (being a corpse-parts conglomeration can do that to you), and how he killed the boy out of revenge. In short, he's pissed off that his maker created him to be alone and miserable. He tells a story about a family of cottagers who gave him hope that he would find compassion, but how even they drove him away. He lost his last chance to connect with society. The monster asks Victor to create for him a female companion as monstrous as he. After much persuading, Victor agrees. At this point, the story is being told by the monster, as told by Victor, as told by Walton.

Victor leaves to make a new monster. He drops off Henry in Scotland while he goes to an island in the Orkneys to work. When he is almost finished, he destroys the second monster, believing he has been tricked by the first monster and that the two will bring destruction to humanity rather than love each other harmlessly. The monster sees him do this and swears revenge…again. Adding insult to injury, Victor throws the pieces of she-monster into the sea. When Victor lands on a shore among Irish people, they accuse him of murdering Henry, who has been found dead. Victor falls ill again. His father comes to visit. When he recovers, he is acquitted with the help of a sympathetic magistrate.

Victor returns to Geneva and prepares to marry Elizabeth before remembering the monster's promise to be with him on his wedding night. Victor thinks the monster is threatening *him*, but the night he and Elizabeth are married, the monster kills the bride instead. This death causes Victor's father to pass away from grief (as he just lost a daughter-in-law and a daughter).

Victor is as alone as the monster, and now, as bent on revenge. We can't really tell the two of them apart anymore except that the monster is taller. And he has some funny-looking joints. Victor chases the monster over all imaginable terrain until he is ragged and near death. That's about the time he gets to Walton's ship. After telling his story, Victor dies. The monster comes aboard the ship, and Walton discovers him crying over the dead body of Victor. He has nothing more to live for, he says, so he goes off to die.

Preface

- Percy Bysshe Shelley, the author's husband, actually wrote the preface. Mary Shelley signed it. Which is so NOT plagiarism.
- It was rainy and kind of creepy the summer Shelley and her husband were vacationing in the Swiss Alps, so they told German ghost stories to pass the time.
- They decided to have a ghost-story contest, and this novel began then.
- There's some name dropping of Dr. Darwin. Not the famous one, but his grandpa, who was a less noteworthy science geek.

Letter 1

- Captain Robert Walton of England is on an expedition to the North Pole. He writes a series of letters to his sister, Margaret to pass the time, and, you know, keep in touch.
- Walton has some goals: see new places, walk where no man has walked before, etc.

Letter 2

- Walton tells his sister that he has no friends. He won't be friends with the men on the ship, either, because they are, um, not as awesome as he. We think we know why he has no friends.
- Walton is lonely. No one could possibly understand him because he's special and more sensitive than the other men. English majors would probably call him a Romantic figure.

Letter 3

- The ship sets sail.

- Walton is overly confident in his outlook for the trip. Since things are going well, something bad is probably going to happen soon.

Letter 4

- Something bad happens! The ship is stuck in sheets of ice in the ocean.
- The crew sees a giant figure in the distance going across the ice on a "sledge," whatever that is. We're thinking "dog sled."
- The next day the ship crew finds another man on yet another sledge. Unfortunately for said man, all but one of his dogs are dead. This man also looks like he has one foot and possibly half a leg in the grave.
- So the crew brings the new guy on board the ship, rubs his body with brandy, and gets him drunk to warm him up. This was back before they knew about alcohol, and how it actually lowers your body temperature.
- Walton wants the new guy all to himself to be the friend he's dreamed of having, which is weirdly possessive.
- At the end of this letter, he tells his sister that the man is going to tell *his* story the next day.

Chapter One

- The new guy's name is Victor Frankenstein. He's just about on his deathbed from starvation, exhaustion, and illness.
- Even though he's half-dead, he still likes to talk, a lot. Instead of just saying, "Hey, my name is Victor. I created a monster, and now I'm trying to kill him because he killed everyone I know," he has to start with the beginning of his childhood:
- "To begin my life with the beginning of my life, I record that I was born" style. Get ready.
- He's got parents. They are named Alphonse and Caroline.
- Then there is Elizabeth. Elizabeth Lavenza. Mary Shelley couldn't really make up her mind about how she became part of Victor's family, but we're guessing you are probably reading the 1831 edition of this novel, so we'll say she was adopted from some Italian family by Caroline when Victor was all of five-years-old.
- Victor's parents thought it would be a good idea to adopt a girl to be Victor's future wife.
- Lucky for Victor, Elizabeth is hot. So Elizabeth comes back to Geneva to live with Victor's family.
- Victor is pretty much accepting of this fate. In general, if something is fate, Victor is ready to give in to it. And, as you are about to see, he seems to think an awful lot of things are fate.

Chapter Two

- Unlike Walton, Victor has friends. Two of them. Or at least, he did during his childhood. First, there is Elizabeth. Victor also has a friend named Henry Clerval.
- Victor describes his idyllic childhood, but don't worry: less happy things are coming. Begin use of historical present.
- As a brooding teenager, Victor develops an interest in science. Especially interesting to him is the old, not to mention discredited, field of alchemy.
- He talks a lot about some guy named Albertus Magnus, who was a real scientist, by the way.
- Victor realizes that science is very powerful, but possibly also destructive, when he sees a tree get struck by lightning. Hmm!

Chapter Three

- Elizabeth catches scarlet fever. She would have died if their mother has not nursed her back to health. Elizabeth recovers, but Caroline catches the illness and dies herself. Really bad things begin here.
- On her deathbed, she tells Victor and Elizabeth she wants them to get married.
- A few weeks later, Victor goes away to study at a university called Ingolstadt. He's only seventeen.
- Once he gets there, he finds a place to live and starts chatting up professors. Some guy named M. Krempe teaches natural philosophy and basically discredits alchemy entirely, to Victor's dismay. Imagine studying all through high school only to get to college and have your teachers tell you that everything you know is wrong and stupid.
- Luckily, Victor meets a nice chemistry professor named Waldman and decides to study science. The real kind.

Chapter Four

- Victor becomes a huge nerd. He doesn't make friends. He doesn't write home, not even to his hot sister/future wife, Elizabeth.
- On the plus side, Victor's studies advance rapidly, which tends to happen when you're in self-prescribed social exile. Soon, he has mastered everything there possibly is to know in the world.
- He becomes obsessed with the way some things are alive and others…aren't really. He wants to figure out how to make non-living things into living ones.
- From a psychological perspective, this probably has something to do with the fact that Victor's mother just died. This is not a healthy alternative to counseling.
- Victor studies anatomy to learn about how bodies live and die.
- He decides he wants to make a new race of creatures, and in his spare time he starts assembling pieces of corpses. No one mentions this, but it probably smells really bad at his

place.

- Further, no one seems too worried about where Victor is getting all the pieces of corpses to sew together. Are we the only curious ones?
- Obsession becomes Victor's middle name.

Chapter Five

- On a dark and stormy night… no seriously, that's in the book. Anyway, on a foreboding night, Victor brings the stitched up corpse pieces to life.
- Victor is on the brink of the achievement of a lifetime. He has visions of a Nobel Prize in Potentially Evil and Highly Suspect Late-Night Doings. He has created a superior race of people. He is going to win fame and adoration and, oh wait. No! The monster is huge and not exactly aesthetically pleasing.
- Victor is roughly thinking, "uh-oh."
- But wait, you say. What's so bad about this monster? Does he club baby seals or throw soda cans in the trash instead of recycling them? Did he hit someone's mother? Nope. Nope. Nope. He's just ugly. That's it.
- And frankly, who did Victor expect from a pile of corpse parts, Brad Pitt? And isn't beauty supposed to be on the inside? But in this story, beautiful = good, ugly = evil. Got it? Take it up with Shelley. Or societal ideals of the 1800s.
- The monster leans over Victor and smiles at him. Oh, the horror.
- But Victor has just had a nightmare about Elizabeth and his mother's corpses (think foreshadowing), so when he sees the ugly smile, he runs out of his house and spends the night in his courtyard.
- The next morning, Victor goes for a walk. He can't seem to be able to stand being in the same room as someone who is ugly.
- In town, in one of many remarkably convenient coincidences in this book, Victor runs into his dear old buddy Henry near the town inn. Henry has come to study at Ingolstadt. It's the thing to do.
- Don't worry – Henry is attractive. So it's okay for Victor to be friends with him.
- Victor immediately falls ill with a fever, and Henry nurses him back to health over a number of months. Illnesses lasted a long time back then because they didn't have things like penicillin or hygiene.
- When Victor recovers, Henry gives him some letters from Elizabeth.

Chapter Six

- Elizabeth is worried about Victor's illness. We are reminded that Victor has at least one good thing going for him right now.
- She also nags Victor to write home. Eventually, he does.
- She also tells him about a girl named Justine who has come to live with their family (as a servant) in Geneva after her own mother's death.

- Victor finally recovers…several months after the shock of seeing something ugly. ✓
- Henry and Victor both start studying "Oriental" languages in school. Victor tries to avoid all the science people. They think he is being modest, but he can't stand to look at them or talk to them because they remind him of the huge mistake he has made.
- He decides to return to Geneva. Before he does, he and Henry go for a walk in nature and appreciate how beautiful it is. Perhaps we would even call it sublime. Hmm! Nature is beautiful…there's something unnatural about the ugly creature…

Chapter Seven

- Back at school, Victor gets a letter from Dad. It seems that someone has murdered his little brother, William. He leaves for Geneva immediately. *R I P*
- Victor arrives too late – the gates of the city have been closed for the night.
- Victor lurks around the woods near where his brother was killed.
- He sees the monster he created for a moment and it occurs to him that, since the monster isn't attractive, he probably committed the murder. No one else has seen this monster or knows anything about it.
- At home the next day (the gates have been opened by now), Victor finds out that Justine has been accused of the murder because she has a picture of Caroline in her pocket – the same picture William had with him right before he died.
- Victor and Elizabeth are the only ones who think Justine is innocent. Well, Justine, too.
- But coward that he is, Victor won't tell anyone why. He's afraid to be labeled a crazy person.

Chapter Eight

- Shocking! Justine confesses even though she is innocent so that she won't go to Hell.
- Elizabeth and Victor still believe in her innocence, although no one else does. Again, except for Justine.
- Justine is executed. *R I P (2)*
- Victor feels stupid. And guilty. His secret has now caused two people he loves to die.

Chapter Nine

- Victor continues to feel 1) stupid and 2) guilty. He mopes around, contemplating suicide.
- His father takes the family to Belrive to try to put the past behind them.
- Victor goes off by himself to the valley of Chamounix and feels momentary happiness due to how beautiful it is (again with the beautiful nature bit – pay attention), but the feeling passes.

Chapter Ten

- Victor feels awful. Then it rains.
- He goes up to the top of Montanvert to see the views, since pretty things have a way of cheering him up.
- Instead he sees the monster.
- Victor threatens to essentially kick the monster's butt, but the monster looks like The Rock.
- The monster, despite everything, invites Victor to come to a cave to talk with him by a fire. FIRE. Look out for that Prometheus reference.
- The monster talks eloquently, so Victor consents to listen to the his life story. We know what you're thinking. Uh-oh – are we in for another "Chapter One: I am Born?" No. This guy is a lot more interesting than Victor.

Chapter Eleven

- The monster relates how he slowly learned about the world through his senses. He also discovered both the benefits of fire (warmth) and its drawbacks (that burning sensation).
- Begin use of historical present.
- At first, the monster attempts to get food by going into a hut, but the inhabitants scream in fear and run out. The same thing happens to him every time he goes into a village, or actually, any dwelling of people anywhere.
- The monster realizes that everyone is prejudiced against him because he is ugly.
- Finally, he finds a small hovel near a cottage and settles in there, watching the family, which consists of a blind old man, and two younger people.

Chapter Twelve

- The monster stays in the hovel all winter. He kind of grows fond of the family he is watching. In fact, he really cares about them.
- At first, he steals food from them, but when he realizes they are poor, he stops and finds food in the woods instead. He also does work at night, like clearing snow or gathering them firewood, just to help them out.
- Why? Because he's a genuine, nice guy. Seriously. The monster is one of the kindest, most helpful people we see in this book.
- He learns that the two younger people are named Felix and Agatha. The monster also realizes they can talk, and he listens to them until he learns their language.
- The monster thinks they are beautiful, and he gets really upset when he looks at his reflection in a pond and remembers how hideous he is. Poor guy. It's really not his fault he's ugly.

Delix ~Agath language

- He feels increasingly isolated, especially when he sees that everyone around him seems to have someone.

Chapter Thirteen

- Because the monster is all sensitive and stuff, he starts to realize that Felix is totally sad, too.
- Soon, a hot, foreign woman arrives at the cottage. Felix perks up. So does everyone else.
- The woman, Safie, doesn't speak the language that the rest of the cottage people do, so they teach it to her. The monster eagerly eavesdrops on her lessons and learns the language, too. He also learns to read.
- He learns about history from the book *Ruins of Empires* that Felix uses to teach Safie.
- The monster's increasing literacy and knowledge is both good and bad; it brings him an understanding of the world he's in, but it reminds him that he can't really participate in the world. He's ugly and different, and now he *really* knows it. And he's alone, and he *really* knows that, too.

Chapter Fourteen

- The monster eavesdrops on the family all the time. Now that he understands what they're saying, he puts together their story, which in many ways is like what has happened to Victor's family.
- Safie's Turkish father was accused wrongly of a crime, much like Justine, and sentenced to death. Safie wanted to marry a European man because Turkish men treat women too much like property, a supposed product of them being Muslim, and her Christian mother taught her that that was a raw deal. Luckily, she met Felix when he was visiting her father in prison, and they fell in love.
- Agatha, Felix, and the blind old man (named De Lacey) were at one time respected and rich Parisians. Felix plotted to help Safie's father escape from prison, but he was discovered, and the family was exiled *sans* all their money.
- Safie's father tried to force her to move to Constantinople, but she escaped to Felix.
- These stories give the monster hope that Felix and De Lacey will be compassionate towards him, since they too have suffered injustice. Not only is the monster kind, but he seems to have quite a sophisticated understanding of the human psyche.

Chapter Fifteen

- (We are still inside the monster's story to Victor.)
- The monster finds books and clothes in the woods one night while he is foraging for food. The most important book for him is *Paradise Lost*, which the monster mistakenly reads as

history instead of fiction. How would he know? He sympathizes with Satan's character. Interesting.

- Since the monster can read, he also finds some of Victor's journal entries in the pockets of the clothes he initially took from Victor. He discovers that Victor was totally grossed out by him and hated that he had brought the monster to life. This stings considerably.
- The monster decides that his last hope for social acceptance lies with the cottagers. Since De Lacey is blind and the younger people often leave him alone during the day, the monster hopes that he can gain De Lacey's trust and acceptance and in turn be trusted by Felix, Agatha, and Safie.
- Soon, the monster gets his opportunity. He approaches De Lacey, who is kind and cordial to him. As bad luck would have it, the others return too soon, and Felix drives the monster away.
- When the monster comes back, the family has moved out.

Chapter Sixteen

- Seeing as everyone hates him for no fair reason, the monster swears revenge on all people, particularly that jerk who created him only to live miserably, ugly, and alone.
- Still, he shows his compassion by rescuing a little girl who slips into a stream and almost drowns. He's a hero, see?
- But when the man accompanying the girl sees the rescue, he assumes the monster is attacking the girl and shoots him. Not the nicest way to say "thank you."
- The monster hides out in the woods, nursing his wounded shoulder. Things are not going so well for him.
- In another occurrence of astounding coincidence, the monster makes it to Geneva and runs into William Frankenstein, Victor's younger brother.
- Apparently shallowness runs in the family, because William reacts much the same way Victor did, calling the monster ugly and wretched.
- The monster is about to let this go when William threatens that his father is Alphonse Frankenstein. Bad call. Enraged upon realizing that William is related to his creator, the monster strangles him with his bare hands.
- Afterwards, he takes the picture of Caroline from William's dead hands and puts it in Justine's pocket. We told you he was clever.
- It is after this explanation that the monster asks for Victor to help him out by creating for him a mate so he won't be alone.
- We probably would have buttered up Victor differently than confessing to murdering his brother. Just a thought.

Chapter Seventeen

- Victor refuses the monster's request.
- The monster's pretty smart though, and he changes tactics by saying that Victor *owes* him

a mate. It is his duty as creator. (Think God, Adam, and Eve.) He says it will make him less evil because it is *loneliness* that has made him such a grumpy jerk/murderer.

- The monster promises to take his new mate to a South American jungle and hide away from people for the rest of their lives. Sounds fair.
- Victor bends like a wet noodle. He agrees, convinced by the monster's smooth rhetoric. The monster is thrilled. He's going to have his own girlfriend.
- Still, he doesn't exactly trust Victor-the-Dead-Beat-Dad. So he vows to follow Victor to check in on his progress. He says he'll know when the work is done, which is just a little creepy and ominous.

Chapter Eighteen

- Victor procrastinates.
- Finally he decides to go off to England to work on his project.
- Before he goes, his father notices that Victor seems pretty upset. Only he thinks it's because Victor doesn't want to marry his hot sister Elizabeth anymore. In Victor's defense, she *is* adopted.
- No, Victor is down for the marriage. But first he's gotta make a second monster.
- Victor arranges with his father to leave for two years. Henry goes with him. Uh-oh.

Chapter Nineteen

- Victor can't really work with Henry and the monster breathing down his neck, so he leaves Henry with an acquaintance in Scotland.
- Victor then rushes off to Orkneys, where he can work on his lady monster in solitude.
- Still, this guy has a tough time getting himself to work. He worries that he might just be making another destructive monster who wants to kill even more people.
- Victor spends all his time alone with his half-finished monster and a guilty conscience. We still don't know where he gets the body parts and stuff to make the second creation.

Chapter Twenty

- All Victor really does is work in his little, abandoned shack. He has all the time in the world to think.
- He has the sudden realization that the new monster will have free will. This complicates things. Even if monster #1 agrees to be peaceful, monster #2 might be furiously angry at being made so hideous. She might hate monster #1. Mrs. Monster might very well go on a killing rampage, and then whose fault would that be? It would be Victor's. At least he thinks so.
- AND what if they had monster babies? The thought is too terrible for Victor to even

consider.

- In the middle of his work, with the monster watching through the window, Victor destroys everything. He thinks he's done a good thing. Maybe he has. But he has broken his promise.
- The monster vows to exact revenge on Victor, promising in a very scary way to be with him on his wedding night.
- Unfortunately, one of Victor's main flaws is his obsession with himself. He assumes that the monster intends to kill him on his wedding night, ignoring the much more obvious threat to Elizabeth, despite the fact that the monster has made a habit of killing people Victor loves.
- We call this frustrating. English majors calls it "dramatic irony."
- The next night, Victor gets a letter from Henry. It basically says, "What's taking so long? Let's go already."
- Victor rows out into the ocean, taking the she-monster remains with him and dumping them into the water.
- After deciding NOT to perish at sea, Victor lands in a nearby town, where instead of being treated hospitably, the people accuse him of committing a murder that happened there the night before. This is fitting, since he did sort of just commit a murder. And dump the body into the water.

Chapter Twenty-One

- So, things get worse from there. The town magistrate, Mr. Kirwin, makes Victor look at the body to see if he has some reaction to it.
- Very sadly, the dead guy is Henry. So Victor is accused of murdering Henry, who really got murdered because Victor destroyed the monster's potential wife.
- We also almost forgot how attractive Henry is. So Shelley reminds us.
- Victor falls ill and stays that way for two months.
- Recovered, he finds himself in prison. Not the best way to wake up from a feverish illness.
- Mr. Kirwin is now inexplicably more compassionate towards Victor than before his illness.
- Further, to Victor's surprise, his father comes to see him.
- The court ends up finding Victor innocent of Henry's death. Something about circumstantial evidence and shameless authorial manipulation of the plot.
- The point is, he can now return to Geneva with his father.

Chapter Twenty-Two

- Victor stops to rest in Paris and recover his strength.
- He gets a letter from Elizabeth, asking him if he is in love with someone else. Nope, not the last time he checked.
- He thinks about the monster's threats, still so painfully oblivious to the monster's true intent. He decides to get on with the marriage and fight the monster, win or lose, to be free

of him one way or the other.

- Back in Geneva, he tells Elizabeth that he has a terrible secret. He can't tell her until after they are married. This is never a good sign.
- Elizabeth, however, is unfazed.
- So they get married and go off to a family cottage in pretty much the middle of nowhere.

Chapter Twenty-Three

- The newlyweds go for a walk around at their cottage. Only Victor has more than wedding night jitters. He is just oozing fear about the monster's arrival.
- Inside the cottage, he sends Elizabeth to bed so he can search the house for the monster. This is not how a wedding night is supposed to go down.
- Big mistake. He hears Elizabeth scream. It suddenly hits Victor what we've all know for chapters now: the monster didn't want to kill him. He wanted, and got, Elizabeth.
- The body count has now reached four.
- Poor Victor really hates himself at this point. He goes home to Geneva to tell his father the sad news, and the man drops dead from grief.
- The body count has now reached five.
- Victor is alone and miserable. Just like the monster he created.
- He goes to a magistrate to try and tell him about the monster and Elizabeth's death, but the magistrate doesn't believe him.
- Since Victor has nothing left to live for, he decides to spend the rest of his life hunting down the monster and attempting to kill him.

Chapter Twenty-Four

- The Great Pursuit begins. The monster leaves a trail of clues for Victor to follow, but never allows his creator to get close enough to catch him.
- During his chase, Victor meets Walton. We're back to the story in a story now, where Victor is on the boat with that sensitive, superior guy who writes letters to his sister. Remember?
- Victor asks Walton to keep up after the monster after Victor dies.
- After that, Victor's narrative ends.
- Walton, for some bizarre reason, believes all of Victor's lunatic ravings. He wishes he had known Victor when he was normal, too, because he thinks he would have made a good friend.
- The crew asks Walton if they can head home already, because with the sub-zero temperatures and the stuck-in-the-ice situation, morale has gotten unbearably low.
- Victor berates them for giving up, and they are momentarily moved to agree with him.
- But two days later, they ask again, and Walton is all "Fine. We can go home."
- When the ship is about to return to England, Victor dies. Just like that.
- A few days pass.

- Walton hears strange noises coming from the room where Victor's body is. He finds the monster crying over Victor's body. Exclamation point.
- Walton is surprised. The monster is still ugly, especially when he's crying.
- Walton's pretty nice to the monster, though.
- The monster concludes that now that his maker is dead, he has no more life purpose such as killing Victor's friends or leaving Victor puzzling clues or stalking Victor from afar.
- Now that he has nothing left, the monster decides to build a funeral pyre for himself on a mountaintop and die. He leaves the ship and disappears into the dark.

Themes

Theme of Life, Consciousness, and Existence

As Victor is the creator of his monster, this plot instantly recalls the much broader implications of the human condition and the relationship between man and God. The relationship between Victor and the monster raises many questions as to the meaning of humanity and existence. If the monster is a modern Adam, then it becomes clear that man is alone in a universe with an indifferent God, that the world brings disaster even to the gentle and good. Men are not born evil, yet are made evil by the precondition of the world makes people evil. If the monster is the fallen angel of *Paradise Lost*, and if Victor is the self-sacrificing Christ, then the text asks a whole different collection of questions. In this scenario, evil stops being evil. The monster instead is someone with whom we sympathize and whom we understand. Further, creations have fee will, and that the scope of that free will exceed the bounds of the creator's imagination. This makes the act of creation an inherently risky and even dangerous act, for the creator but also the entire human race. From here, we must question who is the real hero and who is the villain when we consider the monster in relation to Victor.

Questions About Life, Consciousness, and Existence

1. In what ways is Victor like God? In what ways is he not?
2. Does Victor have a responsibility to the monster beyond giving it life? Does every creator have a responsibility to what he creates?
3. In what ways is the monster simply a part of Victor? In what ways is the monster a distinct entity with free agency?
4. Does the monster have free will? What does that mean, anyway?

Chew on Life, Consciousness, and Existence

Responsibility for the monster's unhappiness lies solely on Victor's shoulders.

In *Frankenstein*, Adam and Satan metaphors work together to create in the monster a character that possesses complex qualities of both good and evil.

Theme of Science

Frankenstein is in one sense the literary manifestation of an entire population's fear of scientific advancement. It serves both as a reflection of present times and a warning for the future. In another sense, Shelley doesn't condemn science itself, but rather the abuse and misuse of it by ignorant or irresponsible individuals. Either way, *Frankenstein* would warn us to proceed with caution as we continue to discover and to create.

Questions About Science

1. How is alchemy portrayed in *Frankenstein*? What if we consider Victor's natural philosophy professor? What if we consider the work Victor does in building a monster?
2. What's the difference, in this book, anyway, between "alchemy" and "science"? Does Victor see them as the same thing? Is this the real problem here, that he's calling it "science" when it is clearly not? Or is what he does science after all?
3. What is it about science that is terrifying enough to merit a cautionary tale about obsessively pushing the boundaries of that field?

Chew on Science

Victor considers his creation to be an act of science, while the rest of society deems it unnatural and evil. In fact, *Frankenstein* argues that there is no difference between the two.

Theme of Appearances

In *Frankenstein*, beauty is considered a virtue of the good, while deformity and ugliness are automatically associated with evil. Because of this stigma, the monster's outward defects prevent him from gaining acceptance into a social sphere – even though he is full of compassion and goodness on the inside. Even the monster's attempts to befriend a blind man fail because social stigma against ugliness is so deeply rooted here. This dichotomy of beauty and ugliness as related to good and evil stems from the book's Romantic influences.

Questions About Appearances

1. Shelley devotes some text to describing the beauty of the natural world. What does this have to do with the monster's ugliness? Is he necessarily unnatural because he was created by man? Is he unnatural for some other reason?
2. The monster believes it is his ugliness that keeps him alienated from society. Is he simply a hideous dude, or does he do anything else to alienate himself? Does he murder because he's ugly, or because he's ostracized? Or is he ostracized because he murders? Is he simply fated to be scorned or could he change his life's destiny if he chose to do so?
3. Why do you think goodness is linked to outer beauty and evilness linked to ugliness? How does this relate to the time period in which this book was written? Is this notion *limited* to the time period?
4. How does Elizabeth fit into the attractive/ugly, good/evil paradigm? What about the fact that, even though she is supposed to be fair and beautiful, she is murdered on her wedding

night? What does that say about justice?

Chew on Appearances

The monster is innately evil, but chooses to blame his evildoings on society.

The monster is not innately evil. He becomes evil only after society treats him like he is because his outward appearance is terrifying.

Theme of Revenge

In *Frankenstein*, revenge becomes the solution for both Victor and his monster. While these two characters relentlessly pursue revenge against each other, they stand in contrast to other characters that take up the more Christian virtue of turning the other cheek. Yet it is revenge that ultimately gives both Victor and the monster a continued connection to the world they are destroying for themselves, and it gives them a continued link to each other. Revenge becomes a distorted way of forming a human bond with another person.

Questions About Revenge

1. How does revenge create tragedy in *Frankenstein*?
2. Who starts the revenge cycle, the monster, or Victor? Does it matter who started it? Who finishes it?
3. How does revenge give both the monster and Victor a purpose in life?
4. Near his death, Victor asks Walton to continue the quest for revenge against the monster. Does Walton honor this request in any way? Why or why not?
5. So, the story ends with the monster declaring he's going to do die. But we never actually see that happen. What is the effect of this?

Chew on Revenge

Although revenge forms a very destructive type of bond between the monster and Victor, it ultimately becomes their shared link to humanity and gives them a reason to live.

Victor's desire for revenge for William's death is ultimately what brings about the deaths of Henry, Elizabeth, and his father. Victor is therefore morally responsible for these tragic events.

Theme of Family

In *Frankenstein*, family becomes the counterpart to loneliness, which in turn is the primary impetus for evil. Family is seen as a solution to the destruction that the monster imposes on Victor. He wants a companion, a mate, a person to create for him some anchor in the social world. Further complicating the issue of family are the deaths of parents and children that occur so frequently throughout the book. With all these children dying, the symbolic suggestion is that the future is threatened. In the case of *Frankenstein*, it is threatened by the new world that

Shelley envisions. When the text is taken in the context of its history (the rapid scientific changes occurring during the Industrial Revolution), these symbolic deaths of the past and future gain significance.

Questions About Family

1. What is the significance of the peasant family in relation to the rest of the story?
2. Why is it important that Walton is writing letters to his sister? Would the action have held different significance if he were writing to his wife or a friend? (Think about the other sister figures in this text, as well as the other wife or lover figures.)
3. William's death foreshadows further tragedy in the book. But does it also have meaning in the sense that William is Victor's *brother*? Why is it the brother that's the first to go?
4. This might help with the above question. Then again it might not. Does the monster want to take on a brother role, or a son role, or some other kind of role relative to his creator?

Chew on Family

Victor's mother's death is the impetus for his creating the monster. Because such an event was beyond his control, Victor is morally exonerated from responsibility for the tragedy that follows.

Walton's need for a friend mirror's the need the monster has for a mate. Indeed, the relationships that Shelley portrays are blind to the sex of the characters, dependent on function and not on gender.

Theme of Exploration

Exploration of the physical world serves as a metaphor for intellectual inquiry and discovery. Exploration is portrayed as dangerous and threatening to life, rather than as something simply good and uplifting for humanity. There is a general fear that certain knowledge may be too extensive or dangerous; it may, *Frankenstein* seems to say, bring about the destruction of humanity.

Questions About Exploration

1. Someone said that exploration in *Frankenstein* is a metaphor for the scientific method. True, or not so true? And, of course, *how so?*
2. After Victor dies, Walton gives up on his exploration and returns to England. What's up with that?
3. What is the distinction between exploration and obsession? Why might these two things have such different outcomes? According to *Frankenstein*, can a person be committed to an endeavor without being obsessed?
4. How does the Industrial Revolution effect the tone of this book in regards to scientific exploration?

Chew on Exploration

Walton's desire for geographic exploration has the same potential for catastrophic results as Victor's studies in alchemy and science. Shelley's warning, therefore, extends far further than to purely scientific fields.

Theme of Language and Communication

Frankenstein is full of questions of communication and language. The story itself is built as a story within a story within a story. Letters form the frame for personal narratives. Communication itself is a point of questioning. Language is how we name the world. Yet the monster has no name. He does not fit into the world. There is no way to make sense of him, so he doesn't get a label. We can't name him "hero" or "villain", and likewise Victor can't name him at all. Victor's name, on the other hand, is highly ironic. He is anything but a victor. Yet his name firmly establishes him in certain traditions. The name is an allusion to *Paradise Lost*, aligning him with the figure of God "The Victor". Additionally, the monster's coming into being is transformed once he acquires a language. He is angered into criminal acts because of language, but he also comes to understand his good nature because of it. Language advances his capacities for both good and evil. One does not negate the other. Language at once gives and takes away his humanity.

Questions About Language and Communication

1. How does the first person narrative affect the way we understand what happens to Victor and with whom we sympathize?
2. In what ways are the specific books that the monster reads influential in forming his identity and concept of self?
3. What is the possible significance of Victor's name? How does understanding the meaning behind his name affect the way we read this story?
4. What function does Safie play in terms of the development of communication in this novel? We knew she was there for *something*.

Chew on Language and Communication

Acquiring language not only gives the monster a sense of his own humanity, but it forces him to come to terms with his alienation from society as well. Language possesses the same good and evil duality that the monster does himself.

The namelessness of the monster establishes him as that which cannot be named, and therefore, that which cannot be understood. His namelessness is the reason that he is alienated, rather than his ugliness.

Theme of Compassion and Forgiveness

Most of the characters in *Frankenstein* seem to lack compassion entirely. The monster alone shows compassion and kindness, attributes that are soon ruined by the world around him. *Frankenstein* further questions just how goodness is judged. We are left unable to judge which characters are good, and which are evil. We are left unsure of whom to forgive, who deserves *our* compassion.

Questions About Compassion and Forgiveness

1. Why isn't Victor compassionate towards the monster he has created? Come on – it's just that the thing is ugly. There has to be more to the story here. Do you really think it would have been hunky-dory of the monster looked like Ashton Kutcher?
2. Is Victor responsible for being compassionate toward the monster?
3. In *Frankenstein*, the only person who does a good deed (rescuing a girl from drowning) is shot in the shoulder. What can you infer about Shelley's view of the world?

Chew on Compassion and Forgiveness

The monster is the true protagonist in the novel because he is the only character who feels compassion, and hence, he is the only character the reader can feel compassion for.

Theme of Sacrifice

In *Frankenstein*, self-sacrifice is a god-like characteristic. It becomes the only way that Victor, our tragic, fallen hero, is able to redeem himself at the end of the text. Yet his self-sacrifice also includes the sacrifice of those he loves. It seems more an act of inhumane, self-absorbed, injustice than it does an act of love for humanity. Victor's fears overwhelm his reasoning, and he chooses to be a hero in his own mind rather than preserving the lives of those he loves. In his mind, he is acting for the good of society when he destroys the companion he is making for the monster, but in doing so, he is sacrificing the lives of his family as well as himself.

Questions About Sacrifice

1. Is Victor sacrificing himself or his family when he chooses to destroy the monster?
2. When Victor destroys the monster's mate instead of finishing it, is he truly enacting a self-sacrifice, or is he using self-sacrifice as an excuse to exact revenge on the monster for killing William and making Victor feel so guilty?

Is Victor a Christ figure?

Chew on Sacrifice

Victor's desire to destroy the monster, although in part based on his fears of the new monster's free will, is equally motivated by a selfish desire for revenge against the monster for killing his brother, William.

Theme of Lies and Deceit

Deception in the form of secrecy is one of Victor's fatal flaws. His inability to share his secret about the monster brings the destruction of those he loves. Further, this loss of family and friends causes Victor to lose his attachment to the world. Secrecy ultimately brings about his inability to save himself.

Questions About Lies and Deceit

1. Would Justine's situation have had a different outcome if Victor had been willing to give up his secrecy? If so, is Victor morally at fault for her death?
2. A first person narrative has a way of concealing as it tells, and telling as it hides. What, if anything, is hidden by this first person narrative? What is revealed?
3. Why does Elizabeth consent to marry Victor even though he is keeping a secret from her? Does she die because of his secret, or would she be fated to die, anyway?
4. When Victor tries to tell a magistrate about the monster, no one believes him. Hmmm…What might this imply? Can Victor really be held responsible for keeping his secret if no one would believe him anyway?

Chew on Lies and Deceit

Victor's duplicitous nature is the cause of his downfall.

Quotes

Life, Consciousness, and Existence Quotes

Another circumstance strengthened and confirmed these feelings. Soon after my arrival in the hovel I discovered some papers in the pocket of the dress which I had taken from your laboratory. At first I had neglected them, but now that I was able to decipher the characters in which they were written, I began to study them with diligence. It was your journal of the four months that preceded my creation. You minutely described in these papers every step you took in the progress of your work; this history was mingled with accounts of domestic occurrences. You doubtless recollect these papers. Here they are. Everything is related in them which bears reference to my accursed origin; the whole detail of that series of disgusting circumstances which produced it is set in view; the minutest description of my odious and loathsome person is given, in language which painted your own horrors and rendered mine indelible. I sickened as I read. `Hateful day when I received life!' I exclaimed in agony. `Accursed creator! Why did you form a monster so hideous that even YOU turned from me in disgust? God, in pity, made man beautiful and alluring, after his own image; but my form is a filthy type of yours, more horrid even from the very resemblance. Satan had his companions, fellow devils, to admire and encourage him, but I am solitary and abhorred. (15.8)

Thought: The monster, on discovering that his own creator is horrified by his existence, increasingly despairs about his position in the world. He faces the tragedy of his existence – that he was made human on the inside, but without the capacity for fellowship with others

"Cursed, cursed creator! Why did I live? Why, in that instant, did I not extinguish the spark of existence which you had so wantonly bestowed? I know not; despair had not yet taken possession of me; my feelings were those of rage and revenge. I could with pleasure have destroyed the cottage and its inhabitants and have glutted myself with their shrieks and misery."
(16.1)

Thought: The monster believes that the blame for his suffering lies with his creator's cruelty and indifference rather than with something innate in himself.

"You are in the wrong," replied the fiend; "and instead of threatening, I am content to reason with you. I am malicious because I am miserable. Am I not shunned and hated by all mankind? You, my creator, would tear me to pieces and triumph; remember that, and tell me why I should pity man more than he pities me? You would not call it murder if you could precipitate me into one of those ice-rifts and destroy my frame, the work of your own hands. Shall I respect man when he condemns me? Let him live with me in the interchange of kindness, and instead of injury I would bestow every benefit upon him with tears of gratitude at his acceptance. But that cannot be; the human senses are insurmountable barriers to our union. Yet mine shall not be the submission of abject slavery. I will revenge my injuries; if I cannot inspire love, I will cause fear, and chiefly towards you my archenemy, because my creator, do I swear inextinguishable hatred. Have a care; I will work at your destruction, nor finish until I desolate your heart, so that you shall curse the hour of your birth." (17.5)

Thought: The monster believes that a female companion is his only chance for happiness.

I was dependent on none and related to none. The path of my departure was free, and there was none to lament my annihilation. My person was hideous and my stature gigantic. What did this mean? Who was I? What was I? Whence did I come? What was my destination? These questions continually recurred, but I was unable to solve them. (15.5)

Thought: The monster is unable to make sense of his own existence; he is unable to find his place in the world and his link to humanity.

Sometimes I allowed my thoughts, unchecked by reason, to ramble in the fields of Paradise, and dared to fancy amiable and lovely creatures sympathizing with my feelings and cheering my gloom; their angelic countenances breathed smiles of consolation. But it was all a dream; no Eve soothed my sorrows nor shared my thoughts; I was alone. I remembered Adam's supplication to his Creator. But where was mine? He had abandoned me, and in the bitterness of my heart I cursed him. (15.11)

Thought: The monster dreams of the companionship and love of his creator, but also feels deep bitterness because he has been abandoned by his own God

The innocent and helpless creature bestowed on them by heaven, whom to bring up to good, and whose future lot it was in their hands to direct to happiness or misery, according as they fulfilled their duties towards me. (1.6)

Thought: Victor, by his own admission, claims that it is the creator's duty to "bring up to good" his own creations. This indicates that his neglect of the monster and the subsequent violence is a reflection of his – Victor's – failures.

Science Quotes

I feel exquisite pleasure in dwelling on the recollections of childhood, before misfortune had tainted my mind and changed its bright visions of extensive usefulness into gloomy and narrow reflections upon self. Besides, in drawing the picture of my early days, I also record those events which led, by insensible steps, to my after tale of misery, for when I would account to myself for the birth of that passion which afterwards ruled my destiny I find it arise, like a mountain river, from ignoble and almost forgotten sources; but, swelling as it proceeded, it became the torrent which, in its course, has swept away all my hopes and joys. Natural philosophy is the genius that has regulated my fate; I desire, therefore, in this narration, to state those facts which led to my predilection for that science. When I was thirteen year of age we all went on a party of pleasure to the baths near Thonon; the inclemency of the weather obliged us to remain a day confined to the inn. In this house I chanced to find a volume of the works of Cornelius Agrippa. I opened it with apathy; the theory which he attempts to demonstrate and the wonderful facts which he relates soon changed this feeling into enthusiasm. A new light seemed to dawn upon my mind, and bounding with joy, I communicated my discovery to my father. My father looked carelessly at the title page of my book and said, "Ah! Cornelius Agrippa! My dear Victor, do not waste your time upon this; it is sad trash." (2.6)

Thought: Victor learns that his interest in alchemy is useless and that such a field is outdated. Instead, science and natural philosophy are the accepted forms of thought.

After having made a few preparatory experiments, he concluded with a panegyric upon modern chemistry, the terms of which I shall never forget: "The ancient teachers of this science," said he, "promised impossibilities and performed nothing. The modern masters promise very little; they know that metals cannot be transmuted and that the elixir of life is a chimera but these philosophers, whose hands seem only made to dabble in dirt, and their eyes to pore over the microscope or crucible, have indeed performed miracles. They penetrate into the recesses of nature and show how she works in her hiding-places. They ascend into the heavens; they have discovered how the blood circulates, and the nature of the air we breathe. They have acquired new and almost unlimited powers; they can command the thunders of heaven, mimic the earthquake, and even mock the invisible world with its own shadows. (3.14)

Thought: This professor of Victor's gives him a way to see scientific inquiry as stemming from older traditions. This respect for the old combined with an interest in the new is what allows Victor to go forward in his scientific explorations.

Appearances Quotes

They consulted their village priest, and the result was that Elizabeth Lavenza became the inmate of my parents' house--my more than sister--the beautiful and adored companion of all my occupations and my pleasures. (1.6)

Thought: Elizabeth's outward beauty is a sign of her inner goodness.

Everyone loved Elizabeth. The passionate and almost reverential attachment with which all regarded her became, while I shared it, my pride and my delight. On the evening previous to her being brought to my home, my mother had said playfully, "I have a pretty present for my Victor--tomorrow he shall have it." And when, on the morrow, she presented Elizabeth to me as her promised gift, I, with childish seriousness, interpreted her words literally and looked upon Elizabeth as mine--mine to protect, love, and cherish. All praises bestowed on her I received as made to a possession of my own. We called each other familiarly by the name of cousin. No word, no expression could body forth the kind of relation in which she stood to me--my more than sister, since till death she was to be mine only. (1.7)

Thought: Victor sees that Elizabeth's beauty is the reason people love her. Yet this seems to be the reason he loves her himself.

As I stood at the door, on a sudden I beheld a stream of fire issue from an old and beautiful oak which stood about twenty yards from our house; and so soon as the dazzling light vanished, the oak had disappeared, and nothing remained but a blasted stump. When we visited it the next morning, we found the tree shattered in a singular manner. It was not splintered by the shock, but entirely reduced to thin ribbons of wood. I never beheld anything so utterly destroyed. (2.9)

Thought: The natural world is at once beautiful and capable of immense destruction.

The summer months passed while I was thus engaged, heart and soul, in one pursuit. It was a most beautiful season; never did the fields bestow a more plentiful harvest or the vines yield a more luxuriant vintage, but my eyes were insensible to the charms of nature. And the same feelings which made me neglect the scenes around me caused me also to forget those friends who were so many miles absent, and whom I had not seen for so long a time. I knew my silence disquieted them, and I well remembered the words of my father: "I know that while you are pleased with yourself you will think of us with affection, and we shall hear regularly from you. You must pardon me if I regard any interruption in your correspondence as a proof that your other duties are equally neglected." (4.10)

Thought: The beauty of nature distracts Victor from his other worries. Nature's beauty has the capacity to alter human feelings

How can I describe my emotions at this catastrophe, or how delineate the wretch whom with such infinite pains and care I had endeavoured to form? His limbs were in proportion, and I had selected his features as beautiful. Beautiful! Great God! His yellow skin scarcely covered the work of muscles and arteries beneath; his hair was of a lustrous black, and flowing; his teeth of a pearly whiteness; but these luxuriances only formed a more horrid contrast with his watery eyes, that seemed almost of the same colour as the dun-white sockets in which they were set, his shrivelled complexion and straight black lips. (5.2)

Thought: Victor's attempt to create a beautiful creature fails.

I had desired it with an ardour that far exceeded moderation; but now that I had finished, the beauty of the dream vanished, and breathless horror and disgust filled my heart. Unable to endure the aspect of the being I had created, I rushed out of the room and continued a long time traversing my bed-chamber, unable to compose my mind to sleep. At length lassitude succeeded to the tumult I had before endured, and I threw myself on the bed in my clothes, endeavouring to seek a few moments of forgetfulness. But it was in vain; I slept, indeed, but I was disturbed by the wildest dreams. I thought I saw Elizabeth, in the bloom of health, walking in the streets of Ingolstadt. Delighted and surprised, I embraced her, but as I imprinted the first kiss on her lips, they became livid with the hue of death; her features appeared to change, and I thought that I held the corpse of my dead mother in my arms; a shroud enveloped her form, and I saw the grave-worms crawling in the folds of the flannel. I started from my sleep with horror; a cold dew covered my forehead, my teeth chattered, and every limb became convulsed; when, by the dim and yellow light of the moon, as it forced its way through the window shutters, I beheld the wretch --the miserable monster whom I had created. He held up the curtain of the bed; and his eyes, if eyes they may be called, were fixed on me. His jaws opened, and he muttered some inarticulate sounds, while a grin wrinkled his cheeks. He might have spoken, but I did not hear; one hand was stretched out, seemingly to detain me, but I escaped and rushed downstairs. I took refuge in the courtyard belonging to the house which I inhabited, where I remained during the rest of the night, walking up and down in the greatest agitation, listening attentively, catching and fearing each sound as if it were to announce the approach of the demoniacal corpse to which I had so miserably given life. (5.3)

Thought: The beauty of Elizabeth and the goodness for which it stands are threatened by Victor's scientific endeavors and the ugly thing he has created.

I wept like a child. "Dear mountains! my own beautiful lake! how do you welcome your wanderer? Your summits are clear; the sky and lake are blue and placid. Is this to prognosticate peace, or to mock at my unhappiness?" (7.20)

Thought: Nature has the power to evoke strong emotions because of its beauty.

During this short voyage I saw the lightning playing on the summit of Mont Blanc in the most beautiful figures. The storm appeared to approach rapidly, and, on landing, I ascended a low hill, that I might observe its progress. It advanced; the heavens were clouded, and I soon felt the rain coming slowly in large drops, but its violence quickly increased. (7.22)

Thought: Beauty and violence are contained together in the natural world.

While I watched the tempest, so beautiful yet terrific, I wandered on with a hasty step. This noble war in the sky elevated my spirits; I clasped my hands, and exclaimed aloud, "William, dear angel! this is thy funeral, this thy dirge!" As I said these words, I perceived in the gloom a figure which stole from behind a clump of trees near me; I stood fixed, gazing intently: I could not be mistaken. A flash of lightning illuminated the object, and discovered its shape plainly to me; its gigantic stature, and the deformity of its aspect more hideous than belongs to humanity, instantly informed me that it was the wretch, the filthy daemon, to whom I had given life. What did he there? Could he be (I shuddered at the conception) the murderer of my brother? (7.24)

Thought: The hideousness of the monster's crime is reflected by the tempestuous weather.

The appearance of Justine was calm. She was dressed in mourning, and her countenance, always engaging, was rendered, by the solemnity of her feelings, exquisitely beautiful. Yet she appeared confident in innocence and did not tremble, although gazed on and execrated by thousands, for all the kindness which her beauty might otherwise have excited was obliterated in the minds of the spectators by the imagination of the enormity she was supposed to have committed. She was tranquil, yet her tranquillity was evidently constrained; and as her confusion had before been adduced as a proof of her guilt, she worked up her mind to an appearance of courage. When she entered the court she threw her eyes round it and quickly discovered where we were seated. A tear seemed to dim her eye when she saw us, but she quickly recovered herself, and a look of sorrowful affection seemed to attest her utter guiltlessness. (8.2)

Thought: Justine's innocence is reflected in her beauty; unlike the monster, her looks reveal her true nature.

Darkness had no effect upon my fancy, and a churchyard was to me merely the receptacle of bodies deprived of life, which, from being the seat of beauty and strength, had become food for the worm. Now I was led to examine the cause and progress of this decay and forced to spend days and nights in vaults and charnel-houses. My attention was fixed upon every object the most insupportable to the delicacy of the human feelings. (4.3)

Thought: The beauty of the church is juxtaposed with the ugliness and decay of death.

Justine, you may remember, was a great favourite of yours; and I recollect you once remarked that if you were in an ill humour, one glance from Justine could dissipate it, for the same reason that Ariosto gives concerning the beauty of Angelica--she looked so frank-hearted and happy. My aunt conceived a great attachment for her, by which she was induced to give her an education superior to that which she had at first intended. This benefit was fully repaid; Justine was the most grateful little creature in the world: I do not mean that she made any professions I never heard one pass her lips, but you could see by her eyes that she almost adored her protectress. Although her disposition was gay and in many respects inconsiderate, yet she paid the greatest attention to every gesture of my aunt. She thought her the model of all excellence and endeavoured to imitate her phraseology and manners, so that even now she often reminds me of her. (6.5)

Thought: Justine's beautiful countenance is representative of her happy, good nature.

Do you understand this feeling? This breeze, which has traveled from the regions towards which I am advancing, gives me a foretaste of those icy climes. Inspirited by this wind of promise, my daydreams become more fervent and vivid. I try in vain to be persuaded that the pole is the seat of frost and desolation; it ever presents itself to my imagination as the region of beauty and delight. There, Margaret, the sun is forever visible, its broad disk just skirting the horizon and diffusing a perpetual splendour. (Letter 1.2)

Thought: The beauty of the natural world inspires Walton to continue in his expedition.

Justine has just returned to us; and I assure you I love her tenderly. She is very clever and gentle, and extremely pretty; as I mentioned before, her mein and her expression continually remind me of my dear aunt. (6.7)

Thought: Justine's beauty makes her an object worth loving.

I must say also a few words to you, my dear cousin, of little darling William. I wish you could see him; he is very tall of his age, with sweet laughing blue eyes, dark eyelashes, and curling hair. When he smiles, two little dimples appear on each cheek, which are rosy with health. He has already had one or two little WIVES, but Louisa Biron is his favourite, a pretty little girl of five years of age. (6.8)

Thought: William's attractiveness is equated with the affection people feel for him.

During our walk, Clerval endeavoured to say a few words of consolation; he could only express his heartfelt sympathy. "Poor William!" said he, dear lovely child, he now sleeps with his angel mother! Who that had seen him bright and joyous in his young beauty, but must weep over his untimely loss! To die so miserably; to feel the murderer's grasp! How much more a murdered that could destroy radiant innocence! Poor little fellow! one only consolation have we; his friends mourn and weep, but he is at rest. The pang is over, his sufferings are at an end for ever. A sod covers his gentle form, and he knows no pain. He can no longer be a subject for pity; we must reserve that for his miserable survivors." (7.16)

Thought: Henry expresses affection for the dead boy by describing his lovely physical attributes.

"He struggled violently. `Let me go,' he cried; `monster! Ugly wretch! You wish to eat me and tear me to pieces. You are an ogre. Let me go, or I will tell my papa.'

"`Boy, you will never see your father again; you must come with me.'

"`Hideous monster! Let me go. My papa is a syndic--he is M. Frankenstein--he will punish you. You dare not keep me.' (16.27-29)

Thought: For William, the monster's ugliness is equated with his being evil.

"As I fixed my eyes on the child, I saw something glittering on his breast. I took it; it was a portrait of a most lovely woman. In spite of my malignity, it softened and attracted me. For a few moments I gazed with delight on her dark eyes, fringed by deep lashes, and her lovely lips; but presently my rage returned; I remembered that I was forever deprived of the delights that such beautiful creatures could bestow and that she whose resemblance I contemplated would, in regarding me, have changed that air of divine benignity to one expressive of disgust and affright. (16.32)

Thought: The monster is upset that normal people will not treat him with kindness merely because he is not attractive.

Her voice was musical but unlike that of either of my friends. On hearing this word, Felix came up hastily to the lady, who, when she saw him, threw up her veil, and I beheld a countenance of angelic beauty and expression. Her hair of a shining raven black, and curiously braided; her eyes were dark, but gentle, although animated; her features of a regular proportion, and her complexion wondrously fair, each cheek tinged with a lovely pink. (13.4)

Thought: Safie's beauty is described as "angelic," indicating that beauty and goodness go hand-in-hand.

Felix seemed ravished with delight when he saw her, every trait of sorrow vanished from his face, and it instantly expressed a degree of ecstatic joy, of which I could hardly have believed it capable; his eyes sparkled, as his cheek flushed with pleasure; and at that moment I thought him as beautiful as the stranger. She appeared affected by different feelings; wiping a few tears from her lovely eyes, she held out her hand to Felix, who kissed it rapturously and called her, as well as I could distinguish, his sweet Arabian. She did not appear to understand him, but smiled. He assisted her to dismount, and dismissing her guide, conducted her into the cottage. Some conversation took place between him and his father, and the young stranger knelt at the old man's feet and would have kissed his hand, but he raised her and embraced her affectionately. (13.5)

Thought: Felix associates beauty and sweetness in Safie.

Oh! No mortal could support the horror of that countenance. A mummy again endued with animation could not be so hideous as that wretch. I had gazed on him while unfinished; he was ugly then, but when those muscles and joints were rendered capable of motion, it became a thing such as even Dante could not have conceived. (5.4)

Thought: The ugly appearance of the monster is likened to something worse than could be found in Dante's description of Hell, further cementing the beautiful-good, ugly-bad dichotomy that destroys the monster's ability to live in society.

The pretty Miss Mansfield has already received the congratulatory visits on her approaching marriage with a young Englishman, John Melbourne, Esq. Her ugly sister, Manon, married M. Duvillard, the rich banker, last autumn. Your favourite schoolfellow, Louis Manoir, has suffered several misfortunes since the departure of Clerval from Geneva. But he has already recovered his spirits, and is reported to be on the point of marrying a lively pretty Frenchwoman, Madame Tavernier. She is a widow, and much older than Manoir; but she is very much admired, and a favourite with everybody. (6.9)

Thought: People admire Madame Tavernier in part because she is good-looking.

I stepped fearfully in: the apartment was empty, and my bedroom was also freed from its hideous guest. I could hardly believe that so great a good fortune could have befallen me, but when I became assured that my enemy had indeed fled, I clapped my hands for joy and ran down to Clerval. (5.12)

Thought: Victor assumes that because his creature is hideous, he must be an enemy.

Of my creation and creator I was absolutely ignorant, but I knew that I possessed no money, no friends, no kind of property. I was, besides, endued with a figure hideously deformed and loathsome; I was not even of the same nature as man. I was more agile than they and could subsist upon coarser diet; I bore the extremes of heat and cold with less injury to my frame; my

stature far exceeded theirs. When I looked around I saw and heard of none like me. Was I, then, a monster, a blot upon the earth, from which all men fled and whom all men disowned? (13.17)

Thought: The monster feels despair over the fact that he cannot be part of man's world simply because he is not good looking.

I admired virtue and good feelings and loved the gentle manners and amiable qualities of my cottagers, but I was shut out from intercourse with them, except through means which I obtained by stealth, when I was unseen and unknown, and which rather increased than satisfied the desire I had of becoming one among my fellows. The gentle words of Agatha and the animated smiles of the charming Arabian were not for me. The mild exhortations of the old man and the lively conversation of the loved Felix were not for me. Miserable, unhappy wretch! (13.19)

Thought: The monster believes he does not get to be happy or receive affection from other people because he is so monstrous.

"It was about seven in the morning, and I longed to obtain food and shelter; at length I perceived a small hut, on a rising ground, which had doubtless been built for the convenience of some shepherd. This was a new sight to me, and I examined the structure with great curiosity. Finding the door open, I entered. An old man sat in it, near a fire, over which he was preparing his breakfast. He turned on hearing a noise, and perceiving me, shrieked loudly, and quitting the hut, ran across the fields with a speed of which his debilitated form hardly appeared capable. His appearance, different from any I had ever before seen, and his flight somewhat surprised me. But I was enchanted by the appearance of the hut; here the snow and rain could not penetrate; the ground was dry; and it presented to me then as exquisite and divine a retreat as Pandemonium appeared to the demons of hell after their sufferings in the lake of fire. I greedily devoured the remnants of the shepherd's breakfast, which consisted of bread, cheese, milk, and wine; the latter, however, I did not like. Then, overcome by fatigue, I lay down among some straw and fell asleep.

It was noon when I awoke, and allured by the warmth of the sun, which shone brightly on the white ground, I determined to recommence my travels; and, depositing the remains of the peasant's breakfast in a wallet I found, I proceeded across the fields for several hours, until at sunset I arrived at a village. How miraculous did this appear! The huts, the neater cottages, and stately houses engaged my admiration by turns. The vegetables in the gardens, the milk and cheese that I saw placed at the windows of some of the cottages, allured my appetite. One of the best of these I entered, but I had hardly placed my foot within the door before the children shrieked, and one of the women fainted. The whole village was roused; some fled, some attacked me, until, grievously bruised by stones and many other kinds of missile weapons, I escaped to the open country and fearfully took refuge in a low hovel, quite bare, and making a wretched appearance after the palaces I had beheld in the village. This hovel however, joined a cottage of a neat and pleasant appearance, but after my late dearly bought experience, I dared not enter it. My place of refuge was constructed of wood, but so low that I could with difficulty sit upright in it. No wood, however, was placed on the earth, which formed the floor, but it was dry;

and although the wind entered it by innumerable chinks, I found it an agreeable asylum from the snow and rain." (11.9-10)

Thought: People reject the monster, although good-natured and kind, simply because he is scary looking.

"I endeavored to crush these fears and to fortify myself for the trial which in a few months I resolved to undergo; and sometimes I allowed my thoughts, unchecked by reason, to ramble in the fields of Paradise, and dared to fancy amiable and lovely creatures sympathizing with my feelings and cheering my gloom; their angelic countenances breathed smiles of consolation. But it was all a dream; no Eve soothed my sorrows nor shared my thoughts; I was alone. I remembered Adam's supplication to his Creator. But where was mine? He had abandoned me, and in the bitterness of my heart I cursed him." (15.11)

Thought: The monster feels as though no one sympathizes with him, as well as recognizes that he has been abandoned by his creator.

"At that instant the cottage door was opened, and Felix, Safie, and Agatha entered. Who can describe their horror and consternation on beholding me? Agatha fainted, and Safie, unable to attend to her friend, rushed out of the cottage. Felix darted forward, and with supernatural force tore me from his father, to whose knees I clung, in a transport of fury, he dashed me to the ground and struck me violently with a stick. I could have torn him limb from limb, as the lion rends the antelope. But my heart sank within me as with bitter sickness, and I refrained. I saw him on the point of repeating his blow, when, overcome by pain and anguish, I quitted the cottage, and in the general tumult escaped unperceived to my hovel." (15.36)

Thought: The monster's last attempt to find a place in society is ruined when the family returns to their blind father.

"I was scarcely hid when a young girl came running towards the spot where I was concealed, laughing, as if she ran from someone in sport. She continued her course along the precipitous sides of the river, when suddenly her foot slipped, and she fell into the rapid stream. I rushed from my hiding-place and with extreme labour, from the force of the current, saved her and dragged her to shore. She was senseless, and I endeavoured by every means in my power to restore animation, when I was suddenly interrupted by the approach of a rustic, who was probably the person from whom she had playfully fled. On seeing me, he darted towards me, and tearing the girl from my arms, hastened towards the deeper parts of the wood. I followed speedily, I hardly knew why; but when the man saw me draw near, he aimed a gun, which he carried, at my body and fired. I sank to the ground, and my injurer, with increased swiftness, escaped into the wood.

This was then the reward of my benevolence! I had saved a human being from destruction, and as a recompense I now writhed under the miserable pain of a wound which shattered the flesh and bone. The feelings of kindness and gentleness which I had entertained but a few moments

before gave place to hellish rage and gnashing of teeth. Inflamed by pain, I vowed eternal hatred and vengeance to all mankind. But the agony of my wound overcame me; my pulses paused, and I fainted." (16.19-20)

Thought: The monster's good deed is not rewarded because people assume he is evil from his appearance.

A fiendish rage animated him as he said this; his face was wrinkled into contortions too horrible for human eyes to behold; but presently he calmed himself and proceeded—(17.6)

Thought: The monster's ugly appearance is equated with fiendishness.

Great God! what a scene has just taken place! I am yet dizzy with the remembrance of it. I hardly know whether I shall have the power to detail it; yet the tale which I have recorded would be incomplete without this final and wonderful catastrophe. I entered the cabin where lay the remains of my ill-fated and admirable friend. Over him hung a form which I cannot find words to describe—gigantic in stature, yet uncouth and distorted in its proportions.

As he hung over the coffin, his face was concealed by long locks of ragged hair; but one vast hand was extended, in colour and apparent texture like that of a mummy. When he heard the sound of my approach, he ceased to utter exclamations of grief and horror and sprung towards the window. Never did I behold a vision so horrible as his face, of such loathsome yet appalling hideousness. I shut my eyes involuntarily and endeavoured to recollect what were my duties with regard to this destroyer. I called on him to stay.

Thought: Walton sees the monster and confirms that he is as terrible looking as Victor said.

Revenge Quotes

When I reflected on his crimes and malice, my hatred and revenge burst all bounds of moderation. I would have made a pilgrimage to the highest peak of the Andes, could I when there have precipitated him to their base. I wished to see him again, that I might wreak the utmost extent of abhorrence on his head and avenge the deaths of William and Justine. Our house was the house of mourning. My father's health was deeply shaken by the horror of the recent events. Elizabeth was sad and desponding; she no longer took delight in her ordinary occupations; all pleasure seemed to her sacrilege toward the dead; eternal woe and tears she then thought was the just tribute she should pay to innocence so blasted and destroyed. She was no longer that happy creature who in earlier youth wandered with me on the banks of the lake and talked with ecstasy of our future prospects. The first of those sorrows which are sent to wean us from the earth had visited her, and its dimming influence quenched her dearest smiles. (9. 6)

Thought: Driven by his inability to forget the past and the deaths he partly caused, Victor seeks revenge on the monster to alleviate his guilty conscience.

I, not in deed, but in effect, was the true murderer. Elizabeth read my anguish in my countenance, and kindly taking my hand, said, "My dearest friend, you must calm yourself. These events have affected me, God knows how deeply; but I am not so wretched as you are. There is an expression of despair, and sometimes of revenge, in your countenance that makes me tremble. Dear Victor, banish these dark passions. Remember the friends around you, who centre all their hopes in you. Have we lost the power of rendering you happy? Ah! While we love, while we are true to each other, here in this land of peace and beauty, your native country, we may reap every tranquil blessing--what can disturb our peace?" (9.8)

Thought: Victor's guilt due to the deaths of William and Justine causes him to seek revenge against the monster.

"Cursed, cursed creator! Why did I live? Why, in that instant, did I not extinguish the spark of existence which you had so wantonly bestowed? I know not; despair had not yet taken possession of me; my feelings were those of rage and revenge. I could with pleasure have destroyed the cottage and its inhabitants and have glutted myself with their shrieks and misery. (16.1).

Thought: The monster wants to seek revenge on *all* people for alienating him. His resentment is against humanity as a whole.

"I continued for the remainder of the day in my hovel in a state of utter and stupid despair. My protectors had departed and had broken the only link that held me to the world. For the first time the feelings of revenge and hatred filled my bosom, and I did not strive to control them, but allowing myself to be borne away by the stream, I bent my mind towards injury and death. When I thought of my friends, of the mild voice of De Lacey, the gentle eyes of Agatha, and the exquisite beauty of the Arabian, these thoughts vanished and a gush of tears somewhat soothed me. But again when I reflected that they had spurned and deserted me, anger returned, a rage of anger, and unable to injure anything human, I turned my fury towards inanimate objects. As night advanced I placed a variety of combustibles around the cottage, and after having destroyed every vestige of cultivation in the garden, I waited with forced impatience until the moon had sunk to commence my operations. (16.12)

Thought: Because he is rejected from society, the monster comforts himself with thoughts of revenge.

The nearer I approached to your habitation, the more deeply did I feel the spirit of revenge enkindled in my heart. (16.17)

Thought: The monster's anger at his creator is channeled into revenge.

All was again silent, but his words rang in my ears. I burned with rage to pursue the murderer of my peace and precipitate him into the ocean. I walked up and down my room hastily and perturbed, while my imagination conjured up a thousand images to torment and sting me. Why had I not followed him and closed with him in mortal strife? But I had suffered him to depart, and he had directed his course towards the mainland. I shuddered to think who might be the next victim sacrificed to his insatiate revenge. And then I thought again of his words -- "I WILL BE WITH YOU ON YOUR WEDDING-NIGHT." That, then, was the period fixed for the fulfillment of my destiny. In that hour I should die and at once satisfy and extinguish his malice. The prospect did not move me to fear; yet when I thought of my beloved Elizabeth, of her tears and endless sorrow, when she should find her lover so barbarously snatched from her, tears, the first I had shed for many months, streamed from my eyes, and I resolved not to fall before my enemy without a bitter struggle. (20.16)

Thought: Victor fears the monster's threats about his wedding night, but would rather face the monster than live life in fear.

This letter revived in my memory what I had before forgotten, the threat of the fiend--"I WILL BE WITH YOU ON YOUR WEDDING-NIGHT!" Such was my sentence, and on that night would the daemon employ every art to destroy me and tear me from the glimpse of happiness which promised partly to console my sufferings. On that night he had determined to consummate his crimes by my death. Well, be it so; a deadly struggle would then assuredly take place, in which if he were victorious I should be at peace and his power over me be at an end. If he were vanquished, I should be a free man. Alas! What freedom? Such as the peasant enjoys when his family have been massacred before his eyes, his cottage burnt, his lands laid waste, and he is turned adrift, homeless, penniless, and alone, but free. Such would be my liberty except that in my Elizabeth I possessed a treasure, alas, balanced by those horrors of remorse and guilt which would pursue me until death. (22.14)

Thought: Victor is afraid of pulling Elizabeth into his destructive interactions with the monster, but his obsession will not give him peace.

"Frankenstein! you belong then to my enemy--to him towards whom I have sworn eternal revenge; you shall be my first victim." (16.30)

Thought: The monster decides to kill William because he is related to Victor. He hopes that he can make Victor as alone and miserable as he is himself.

Family Quotes

I shall commit my thoughts to paper, it is true; but that is a poor medium for the communication of feeling. I desire the company of a man who could sympathize with me, whose eyes would reply to mine. You may deem me romantic, my dear sister, but I bitterly feel the want of a friend. I have no one near me, gentle yet courageous, possessed of a cultivated as well as of a capacious mind, whose tastes are like my own, to approve or amend my plans. How would such a friend repair the faults of your poor brother! I am too ardent in execution and too impatient of difficulties. But it is a still greater evil to me that I am self-educated: for the first fourteen years of my life I ran wild on a common and read nothing but our Uncle Thomas' books of voyages. At that age I became acquainted with the celebrated poets of our own country; but it was only when it had ceased to be in my power to derive its most important benefits from such a conviction that I perceived the necessity of becoming acquainted with more languages than that of my native country. Now I am twenty-eight and am in reality more illiterate than many schoolboys of fifteen. It is true that I have thought more and that my daydreams are more extended and magnificent, but they want (as the painters call it) KEEPING; and I greatly need a friend who would have sense enough not to despise me as romantic, and affection enough for me to endeavour to regulate my mind. Well, these are useless complaints; I shall certainly find no friend on the wide ocean, nor even here in Archangel, among merchants and seamen. Yet some feelings, unallied to the dross of human nature, beat even in these rugged bosoms. My lieutenant, for instance, is a man of wonderful courage and enterprise; he is madly desirous of glory, or rather, to word my phrase more characteristically, of advancement in his profession. He is an Englishman, and in the midst of national and professional prejudices, unsoftened by cultivation, retains some of the noblest endowments of humanity. I first became acquainted with him on board a whale vessel; finding that he was unemployed in this city, I easily engaged him to assist in my enterprise. The master is a person of an excellent disposition and is remarkable in the ship for his gentleness and the mildness of his discipline. This circumstance, added to his well-known integrity and dauntless courage, made me very desirous to engage him. A youth passed in solitude, my best years spent under your gentle and feminine fosterage, has so refined the groundwork of my character that I cannot overcome an intense distaste to the usual brutality exercised on board ship: (Letter 2.2)

Thought: Walton's desire for a friend establishes a major thematic meditation of the text: that being alone in the world creates the desire to have a circle of family and friends. This desire of Walton's mirrors the later desire of the monster to have a companion.

When my father returned from Milan, he found playing with me in the hall of our villa a child fairer than pictured cherub--a creature who seemed to shed radiance from her looks and whose form and motions were lighter than the chamois of the hills. The apparition was soon explained. With his permission my mother prevailed on her rustic guardians to yield their charge to her. They were fond of the sweet orphan. Her presence had seemed a blessing to them, but it would be unfair to her to keep her in poverty and want when Providence afforded her such powerful protection. They consulted their village priest, and the result was that Elizabeth Lavenza became the inmate of my parents' house--my more than sister--the beautiful and adored companion of all my occupations and my pleasures. (1.6)

Thought: Although Elizabeth is welcomed into Victor's full, happy family, her status as an orphan reminds us that family that can be destroyed at any moment. The threat of being alone is always present.

No human being could have passed a happier childhood than myself. My parents were possessed by the very spirit of kindness and indulgence. We felt that they were not the tyrants to rule our lot according to their caprice, but the agents and creators of all the many delights which we enjoyed. When I mingled with other families I distinctly discerned how peculiarly fortunate my lot was, and gratitude assisted the development of filial love. (2.3)

Thought: Victor establishes his family as a happy one, and his parents as the bringers of "many delights." Victor knows what a blessing it is to have your creators care about you, yet this knowledge does not compel him to do the same for the creature to whom he gives life.

My departure was therefore fixed at an early date, but before the day resolved upon could arrive, the first misfortune of my life occurred--an omen, as it were, of my future misery. Elizabeth had caught the scarlet fever; her illness was severe, and she was in the greatest danger. During her illness many arguments had been urged to persuade my mother to refrain from attending upon her. She had at first yielded to our entreaties, but when she heard that the life of her favourite was menaced, she could no longer control her anxiety. She attended her sickbed; her watchful attentions triumphed over the malignity of the distemper--Elizabeth was saved, but the consequences of this imprudence were fatal to her preserver. On the third day my mother sickened; her fever was accompanied by the most alarming symptoms, and the looks of her medical attendants prognosticated the worst event. On her deathbed the fortitude and benignity of this best of women did not desert her. She joined the hands of Elizabeth and myself. "My children," she said, "my firmest hopes of future happiness were placed on the prospect of your union. This expectation will now be the consolation of your father. Elizabeth, my love, you must supply my place to my younger children. Alas! I regret that I am taken from you; and, happy and beloved as I have been, is it not hard to quit you all? But these are not thoughts befitting me; I will endeavour to resign myself cheerfully to death and will indulge a hope of meeting you in another world." (3.1)

Thought: The loss of Victor's mother serves as an omen of the loss he is going to encounter again and again as the story progresses. At the same time, her death establishes that family is what is most dear to Victor, what he most sorely does not want to lose.

She died calmly, and her countenance expressed affection even in death. I need not describe the feelings of those whose dearest ties are rent by that most irreparable evil, the void that presents itself to the soul, and the despair that is exhibited on the countenance. It is so long before the mind can persuade itself that she whom we saw every day and whose very existence appeared a part of our own can have departed forever--that the brightness of a beloved eye can have been extinguished and the sound of a voice so familiar and dear to the ear can be hushed, never more to be heard. These are the reflections of the first days; but when the lapse of time proves the reality of the evil, then the actual bitterness of grief commences. Yet from whom has

not that rude hand rent away some dear connection? And why should I describe a sorrow which all have felt, and must feel? The time at length arrives when grief is rather an indulgence than a necessity; and the smile that plays upon the lips, although it may be deemed a sacrilege, is not banished. My mother was dead, but we had still duties which we ought to perform; we must continue our course with the rest and learn to think ourselves fortunate whilst one remains whom the spoiler has not seized. (3.2)

Thought: Loss haunts Victor from a very early point in the book: his mother's death is an "irreparable evil" from which all future evil and loneliness spring.

I lay on my straw, but I could not sleep. I thought of the occurrences of the day. What chiefly struck me was the gentle manners of these people, and I longed to join them, but dared not. I remembered too well the treatment I had suffered the night before from the barbarous villagers, and resolved, whatever course of conduct I might hereafter think it right to pursue, that for the present I would remain quietly in my hovel, watching and endeavouring to discover the motives which influenced their actions. (12.1)

Thought: The monster longs for companionship with the family he observes, but he cannot engage with them because he is unacceptable to society. Instead, he must remain entirely alone.

I had admired the perfect forms of my cottagers--their grace, beauty, and delicate complexions; but how was I terrified when I viewed myself in a transparent pool! At first I started back, unable to believe that it was indeed I who was reflected in the mirror; and when I became fully convinced that I was in reality the monster that I am, I was filled with the bitterest sensations of despondence and mortification. Alas! I did not yet entirely know the fatal effects of this miserable deformity. (12.13)

Thought: The monster refers to the family as "my" cottagers, implying his sense of connection to these people and his desire to be included in their family. Despite this, he knows he suffers the "fatal effects of this miserable deformity" and will be kept separate from them.

My thoughts now became more active, and I longed to discover the motives and feelings of these lovely creatures; I was inquisitive to know why Felix appeared so miserable and Agatha so sad. I thought (foolish wretch!) that it might be in my power to restore happiness to these deserving people. When I slept or was absent, the forms of the venerable blind father, the gentle Agatha, and the excellent Felix flitted before me. I looked upon them as superior beings who would be the arbiters of my future destiny. I formed in my imagination a thousand pictures of presenting myself to them, and their reception of me. I imagined that they would be disgusted, until, by my gentle demeanour and conciliating words, I should first win their favour and afterwards their love. (12.17)

Thought: The monster's desire for love and familial affection makes him a deeply human and sympathetic character. Yet it also drives him to commit his immoral acts.

"You must create a female for me with whom I can live in the interchange of those sympathies necessary for my being. This you alone can do, and I demand it of you as a right which you must not refuse to concede." (17.2)

Thought: The monster's desire for a female companion parallels Adam's asking God for a woman.

Other lessons were impressed upon me even more deeply. I heard of the difference of sexes, and the birth and growth of children, how the father doted on the smiles of the infant, and the lively sallies of the older child, how all the life and cares of the mother were wrapped up in the precious charge, how the mind of youth expanded and gained knowledge, of brother, sister, and all the various relationships which bind one human being to another in mutual bonds. (13.21)

Thought: As the monster learns about the world and becomes educated, he realizes he is utterly alone and alienated from society. He has no "mutual bonds" to anyone – except Victor, who has rejected him.

But where were my friends and relations? No father had watched my infant days, no mother had blessed me with smiles and caresses; or if they had, all my past life was now a blot, a blind vacancy in which I distinguished nothing. From my earliest remembrance I had been as I then was in height and proportion. I had never yet seen a being resembling me or who claimed any intercourse with me. What was I? The question again recurred, to be answered only with groans. (13.22)

Thought: When the monster asks, "What was I?" he acknowledges that he has no role in society. He is the nameless monster because society does not understand him, and he does not fit in – there isn't a word for him, and there are no easy answers to his questions, either.

Exploration Quotes

I cannot describe to you my sensations on the near prospect of my undertaking. It is impossible to communicate to you a conception of the trembling sensation, half pleasurable and half fearful, with which I am preparing to depart. I am going to unexplored regions, to "the land of mist and snow," but I shall kill no albatross; therefore do not be alarmed for my safety or if I should come back to you as worn and woeful as the "Ancient Mariner." You will smile at my allusion, but I will disclose a secret. I have often attributed my attachment to, my passionate enthusiasm for, the dangerous mysteries of ocean to that production of the most imaginative of modern poets. There is something at work in my soul which I do not understand. I am practically industrious-- painstaking, a workman to execute with perseverance and labour--but besides this there is a love for the marvellous, a belief in the marvellous, intertwined in all my projects, which

hurries me out of the common pathways of men, even to the wild sea and unvisited regions I am about to explore. (Letter 2.4)

Thought: Walton describes his desire to travel and explore the world. He is an exploratory person both in terms of physical travel and the mental exploration of intellectual discovery.

But success SHALL crown my endeavours. Wherefore not? Thus far I have gone, tracing a secure way over the pathless seas, the very stars themselves being witnesses and testimonies of my triumph. Why not still proceed over the untamed yet obedient element? What can stop the determined heart and resolved will of man? (Letter 3.4)

Thought: Walton, before his journey, possesses an overwhelming sense of confidence in his abilities. This reveals his lack of forethought about the possibility of danger. He is consumed with his grandiose ambitions in much the same way Victor is when he builds his monster. Only after it is too late does he realize the cost of his intellectual exploration.

My temper was sometimes violent, and my passions vehement; but by some law in my temperature they were turned not towards childish pursuits but to an eager desire to learn, and not to learn all things indiscriminately. I confess that neither the structure of languages, nor the code of governments, nor the politics of various states possessed attractions for me. It was the secrets of heaven and earth that I desired to learn; and whether it was the outward substance of things or the inner spirit of nature and the mysterious soul of man that occupied me, still my inquiries were directed to the metaphysical, or in it highest sense, the physical secrets of the world. (2.4)

Thought: Victor expresses his innate intellectual exploratory nature.

Such were the professor's words – rather let me say such the words of the fate – enounced to destroy me. As he went on I felt as if my soul were grappling with a palpable enemy; one by one the various keys were touched which formed the mechanism of my being; chord after chord was sounded, and soon my mind was filled with one thought, one conception, one purpose. So much has been done, exclaimed the soul of Frankenstein--more, far more, will I achieve; treading in the steps already marked, I will pioneer a new way, explore unknown powers, and unfold to the world the deepest mysteries of creation. (3.15)

Thought: Victor idealizes scientific inquiry without being aware of its dangers. He is treading fearlessly where he should be moving with caution.

I trod heaven in my thoughts, now exulting in my powers, now burning with the idea of their effects. From my infancy I was imbued with high hopes and a lofty ambition. (24.25)

Thought: Ambition and hope are tied to the idea of mental exploration.

I mentioned in my last letter the fears I entertained of a mutiny. This morning, as I sat watching the wan countenance of my friend--his eyes half closed and his limbs hanging listlessly--I was roused by half a dozen of the sailors, who demanded admission into the cabin. They entered, and their leader addressed me. He told me that he and his companions had been chosen by the other sailors to come in deputation to me to make me a requisition which, in justice, I could not refuse. We were immured in ice and should probably never escape, but they feared that if, as was possible, the ice should dissipate and a free passage be opened, I should be rash enough to continue my voyage and lead them into fresh dangers, after they might happily have surmounted this. They insisted, therefore, that I should engage with a solemn promise that if the vessel should be freed I would instantly direct my course southwards. (24.33)

Thought: Walton's crew wants to turn back to England without discovering anything. Although Walton is disappointed by such a prospect, he also starts to view the exploratory mindset in a more negative way due to his interaction with Victor.

The die is cast; I have consented to return if we are not destroyed. Thus are my hopes blasted by cowardice and indecision; I come back ignorant and disappointed. It requires more philosophy than I possess to bear this injustice with patience. (24.37)

Thought: Walton realizes that he would rather have his life than new knowledge. He chooses safety over the dangers of exploration – unlike Victor.

Language and Communication Quotes
My days were spent in close attention, that I might more speedily master the language; and I may boast that I improved more rapidly than the Arabian, who understood very little and conversed in broken accents, whilst I comprehended and could imitate almost every word that was spoken. (13.12)

Thought: The monster demonstrates a facility for language and a natural ability to learn.

Another circumstance strengthened and confirmed these feelings. Soon after my arrival in the hovel I discovered some papers in the pocket of the dress which I had taken from your laboratory. At first I had neglected them, but now that I was able to decipher the characters in which they were written, I began to study them with diligence. It was your journal of the four months that preceded my creation. You minutely described in these papers every step you took in the progress of your work; this history was mingled with accounts of domestic occurrences. You doubtless recollect these papers. Here they are. Everything is related in them which bears reference to my accursed origin; the whole detail of that series of disgusting circumstances which produced it is set in view; the minutest description of my odious and loathsome person is given, in language which painted your own horrors and rendered mine indelible. I sickened as I

read. `Hateful day when I received life!' I exclaimed in agony. `Accursed creator! Why did you form a monster so hideous that even YOU turned from me in disgust? God, in pity, made man beautiful and alluring, after his own image; but my form is a filthy type of yours, more horrid even from the very resemblance. Satan had his companions, fellow devils, to admire and encourage him, but I am solitary and abhorred. (15.8)

Thought: The monster learns of his origin through reading. His new knowledge gives him insight into himself, but it also gives him a sense of personal loss that he didn't have beforehand. Now that he does understand his nature, he realizes the horror of his situation.

And what was I? Of my creation and creator I was absolutely ignorant, but I knew that I possessed no money, no friends, no kind of property. (13.17)

Thought: The monster, in learning language, realizes he has very few words with which to define himself. He struggles here with self-identity.

Compassion and Forgiveness Quotes

These thoughts exhilarated me and led me to apply with fresh ardour to the acquiring the art of language. My organs were indeed harsh, but supple; and although my voice was very unlike the soft music of their tones, yet I pronounced such words as I understood with tolerable ease. It was as the ass and the lap-dog; yet surely the gentle ass whose intentions were affectionate, although his manners were rude, deserved better treatment than blows and execration. (12.18)

Thought: The monster reasons that his inner nature should be the basis for people's judgment of him, rather than his coarse but harmless outer features. He relies on a compassion that is present only in himself. This faulty assumption sets him up for disappointment.

This was then the reward of my benevolence! I had saved a human being from destruction, and as a recompense I now writhed under the miserable pain of a wound which shattered the flesh and bone. The feelings of kindness and gentleness which I had entertained but a few moments before gave place to hellish rage and gnashing of teeth. Inflamed by pain, I vowed eternal hatred and vengeance to all mankind. (16.20)

Thought: Although the monster is compassionate, he learns that others are not. The world is indifferent at best, and hateful and mistrusting at worst.

At this time a slight sleep relieved me from the pain of reflection which was disturbed by the approach of a beautiful child, who came running into the recess I had chosen, with all the sportiveness of infancy. Suddenly, as I gazed on him, an idea seized me that this little creature was unprejudiced and had lived too short a time to have imbibed a horror of deformity. If, therefore, I could seize him and educate him as my companion and friend, I should not be so desolate in this peopled earth.

Urged by this impulse, I seized on the boy as he passed and drew him towards me. As soon as he beheld my form, he placed his hands before his eyes and uttered a shrill scream; I drew his hand forcibly from his face and said, "Child, what is the meaning of this? I do not intend to hurt you; listen to me."

He struggled violently. "Let me go," he cried; "monster! Ugly wretch! You wish to eat me and tear me to pieces. You are an ogre. Let me go, or I will tell my papa." (16.25-27)

Thought: The monster hopes that a young child will not yet have formed such biases against a being based on appearances. Again, his naive presumptions set him up for disappointment.

Sacrifice Quotes

Had I right, for my own benefit, to inflict this curse upon everlasting generations? I had before been moved by the sophisms of the being I had created; I had been struck senseless by his fiendish threats; but now, for the first time, the wickedness of my promise burst upon me; I shuddered to think that future ages might curse me as their pest, whose selfishness had not hesitated to buy its own peace at the price, perhaps, of the existence of the whole human race. (20.1)

Thought: Victor realizes that he must go back on his promise in order to protect humanity from the monster he inadvertently created. He realizes he must give up his own safety and desires in order to protect humanity from the dangers of his intellectual exploration.

"Shall each man," cried he, "find a wife for his bosom, and each beast have his mate, and I be alone? I had feelings of affection, and they were requited by detestation and scorn. Man! You may hate, but beware! Your hours will pass in dread and misery, and soon the bolt will fall which must ravish from you your happiness forever. Are you to be happy while I grovel in the intensity of my wretchedness? You can blast my other passions, but revenge remains -- revenge, henceforth dearer than light or food! I may die, but first you, my tyrant and tormentor, shall curse the sun that gazes on your misery. Beware, for I am fearless and therefore powerful. I will watch with the wiliness of a snake, that I may sting with its venom. Man, you shall repent of the injuries you inflict." (20.11)

Thought: The monster expresses to Victor that he could lose everything if he goes against the monster's wishes. But Victor remains steadfastly self-sacrificing, realizing that the danger to the world is larger than the danger to himself. He is forced to self-sacrifice to account for his hasty rush into scientific inquiry.

Lies and Deceit Quotes

The world was to me a secret which I desired to divine. Curiosity, earnest research to learn the hidden laws of nature, gladness akin to rapture, as they were unfolded to me, are among the earliest sensations I can remember. (2.1)

Thought: The laws of nature are described as a hidden secret.

It was the secrets of heaven and earth that I desired to learn; and whether it was the outward substance of things or the inner spirit of nature and the mysterious soul of man that occupied me, still my inquiries were directed to the metaphysical, or in it highest sense, the physical secrets of the world. (2.4)

Thought: Science is equated with secret knowledge.

I have described myself as always having been imbued with a fervent longing to penetrate the secrets of nature. In spite of the intense labour and wonderful discoveries of modern philosophers, I always came from my studies discontented and unsatisfied. (2.7)

Thought: The secret nature of scientific knowledge prompts Victor's obsessive desire to go deeper in his quest for the secret of life.

I turned my reluctant steps from my father's door--led me first to M. Krempe, professor of natural philosophy. He was an uncouth man, but deeply imbued in the secrets of his science. (3.9)

Thought: Science is again construed as a secretive art.

One of the phenomena which had peculiarly attracted my attention was the structure of the human frame, and, indeed, any animal endued with life. Whence, I often asked myself, did the principle of life proceed? It was a bold question, and one which has ever been considered as a mystery; yet with how many things are we upon the brink of becoming acquainted, if cowardice or carelessness did not restrain our inquiries. I revolved these circumstances in my mind and determined thenceforth to apply myself more particularly to those branches of natural philosophy which relate to physiology. Unless I had been animated by an almost supernatural enthusiasm, my application to this study would have been irksome and almost intolerable. To examine the causes of life, we must first have recourse to death. I became acquainted with the science of anatomy, but this was not sufficient; I must also observe the natural decay and corruption of the human body. In my education my father had taken the greatest precautions that my mind should be impressed with no supernatural horrors. I do not ever remember to have trembled at a tale of superstition or to have feared the apparition of a spirit. Darkness had no effect upon my fancy, and a churchyard was to me merely the receptacle of bodies deprived of life, which, from being the seat of beauty and strength, had become food for the worm. Now I was led to examine the cause and progress of this decay and forced to spend days and nights in vaults and charnel-houses. My attention was fixed upon every object the most insupportable

to the delicacy of the human feelings. I saw how the fine form of man was degraded and wasted; I beheld the corruption of death succeed to the blooming cheek of life; I saw how the worm inherited the wonders of the eye and brain. I paused, examining and analysing all the minutiae of causation, as exemplified in the change from life to death, and death to life, until from the midst of this darkness a sudden light broke in upon me--a light so brilliant and wondrous, yet so simple, that while I became dizzy with the immensity of the prospect which it illustrated, I was surprised that among so many men of genius who had directed their inquiries towards the same science, that I alone should be reserved to discover so astonishing a secret. (4.3)

Thought: Victor discovers the secret to life and feels astonished that he should be the one to figure it out.

Who shall conceive the horrors of my secret toil as I dabbled among the unhallowed damps of the grave or tortured the living animal to animate the lifeless clay? (4.9)

Thought: Victor's obsessive drive to create life forces him into secret "horrors."

I saw plainly that he was surprised, but he never attempted to draw my secret from me; and although I loved him with a mixture of affection and reverence that knew no bounds, yet I could never persuade myself to confide in him that event which was so often present to my recollection, but which I feared the detail to another would only impress more deeply. (6.12)

Thought: Victor feels disconnected from Henry because he is keeping his knowledge as well as his monster a secret.

My father had often, during my imprisonment, heard me make the same assertion; when I thus accused myself, he sometimes seemed to desire an explanation, and at others he appeared to consider it as the offspring of delirium, and that, during my illness, some idea of this kind had presented itself to my imagination, the remembrance of which I preserved in my convalescence.

Thought: The secrecy of Victor's discovery makes him appear crazy to those around him.

I avoided explanation and maintained a continual silence concerning the wretch I had created. I had a persuasion that I should be supposed mad, and this in itself would forever have chained my tongue. But, besides, I could not bring myself to disclose a secret which would fill my hearer with consternation and make fear and unnatural horror the inmates of his breast. I checked, therefore, my impatient thirst for sympathy and was silent when I would have given the world to have confided the fatal secret. Yet, still, words like those I have recorded would burst uncontrollably from me. I could offer no explanation of them, but their truth in part relieved the burden of my mysterious woe. (22.4-5)

Thought: Victor feels that his creation is a secret burden that cannot be relieved.

Plot Analysis

Classic Plot Analysis

Initial Situation
Victor and his family are content, happy-go-lucky, adopting-future-wives-as-sisters kind of people.
This is super boring. We sure hope something happens soon. Something like a conflict.

Conflict
Victor's mother dies.
Victor's way of grieving his mother's death is to get obsessed with death and to bring something dead, or rather, a compilation of many dead somethings, back to life. Adding conflict to conflict, the monster is really, really, ridiculously ugly. By playing God, Victor has gotten more than he had bargained for. He has created this conflict for himself. And now he will suffer for it.

Complication
The monster is unhappy with his life and kills William.
Victor's monster is out of control. This was slightly unexpected. And it complicated matters. Again, this is Victor's own doing; if he hadn't neglected his creation, his creation wouldn't have gone on a killing spree.

Climax
Victor decides to destroy the second monster he is working on.
At this point, Victor makes his pivotal decision. It is the only place in the text since this whole terrible chain of events started where he takes decisive action instead of sitting around whining about how fate is running its course. Once he chooses to destroy said second monster, he sets in motion the final stages of his self-destruction.

Suspense
The monster promises to be with Victor on his wedding night.
We as the reader realize that the monster means he is going to kill Elizabeth, but Victor thinks the monster is going to kill him. This disconnect (fine, "dramatic irony") brings about the most suspenseful part of the book, as we wait to see whether 1) Victor figures it out in time or 2) Elizabeth dies a gruesome death. You get two guesses.

Denouement
Henry, Elizabeth, and Victor's father all die.
Things get wrapped up, but not in a happy way. Everyone dies, which is an efficient but also depressing way to tie up loose ends. Victor's vow to kill the monster counts as denouement and NOT suspense, we think, because we didn't sit around with our hearts racing wondering if

he was going to succeed or not. Maybe it's the way he said it, the sort of "I'm going to spend the rest of my life" bit. It suggests that nothing concrete is going to be happening any time soon. So don't hold your breath.

Conclusion
Victor and the monster both die.
Again, a nifty way to tie up loose ends.

Booker's Seven Basic Plots Analysis: Tragedy

Anticipation Stage
Victor wants to uncover the secret of bringing things to life.
Victor becomes aware of the vast power and destructiveness of nature. He seeks an education at the university of Ingolstadt. Unfortunately his interest in alchemy is unappreciated by his professors. He sets out studying, attempting to uncover the "secret of life," or rather the secret of making corpse pieces move. We think this has something to do with the fact that his mother died quite recently.

Dream Stage
All of Victor's dreams have come true when his scientific endeavors prove fruitful. This lasts about five seconds.
Shortest lived dream stage ever.

Frustration Stage
The monster is scary and ugly instead of wonderful. Also, he kills William. Victor agrees to create a second monster in an attempt to fix his mistake.
The monster isn't what Victor meant to create, but once he has brought the creature to life, he can't undo it. Not to mention, the monster kills William and brings about Justine's death.
We're feeling rather frustrated. This is all Victor's fault and he can't undo it except by giving in to the monster's wish of having a companion. But he's caught between an ugly rock and hard, uglier place: if he makes another monster, things could get worse.

Nightmare Stage
The monster is angry with Victor for destroying what would have been his mate, and he kills Henry and Elizabeth.
Everything goes wrong for Victor. One by one, the monster takes away everyone in Victor's life until he is as lonely as the monster he created. Everyone has to die because Victor screwed up. What a nightmare.

Destruction or Death Wish Stage
Victor chases after the monster and, in a sense, his own death.
Victor's chase after the monster leaves him sick, emaciated, and near death. Once he is aboard Walter's ship, it becomes obvious that Victor has killed himself in his attempt to destroy the monster once and for all. Finally and fittingly, Victor and the monster die.

Three Act Plot Analysis

Act I
Victor creates a monster and abandons it in the world.

Act II
The monster becomes unhappy because no one understands him; he seeks to punish his creator for his abandonment. They both end up alone – except for the relationship they have with one another.

Act III
Victor chases after the monster to kill him. Victor dies, and the monster, realizing he's lost his only companion, goes off to die.

Study Questions

1. Victor doesn't give his monster a name. What does this do for the story? What does it say about us in society today that we think the monster's name is Frankenstein (besides the fact that we are apparently ill-read)?
2. How is science portrayed in *Frankenstein*? Consider that this book was written in the midst of vast scientific advances and the advent of the Industrial Revolution.
3. How would this novel be different if the characters could let go of their need for revenge?
4. You might have noticed some Christian influences in this text. To start off, there's the creator/creation paradigm. And, of course, the monster is compared to Adam. But the monster is also compared to the fallen angel – Satan – and Victor takes on comparisons to God. You could even go so far as to call Victor's death a sacrifice that makes him a Christ figure. Do the book's Christian influences force characters to be either good or evil? What might Shelley be saying about this?
5. Victor does not trust the monster; supposedly, that's why he breaks his promise to create him a companion. Is the monster trustworthy? Can Victory be trustworthy even though he broke his promise?
6. We've identified two major themes. The first is the fear of science. The second is that ugly people get the shaft. The question is, are these related? Do they compliment each other in any way? Why might Shelley have chosen to explore both these topics in the same novel? Or was she just killing two birds with one stone?

Characters

All Characters

Victor Frankenstein Character Analysis

Victor's character is complicated. He grows from a young, innocent, hopeful boy into a jaded, vindictive, vengeful man. Driven by a desire for knowledge and an exploratory nature, Victor's crime is one of obsession. He oversteps the bounds of science in becoming the creator of a being that never should have lived.

His ultimate flaw – aside from being shallow, foolish, and generally unaware of the threats posed to his loved ones – is not providing for the creature to whom he gives life. But that's not all. He is also unable to rectify the consequences of his inquiring mind. He doesn't take responsibility for the monster, ever. He goes back on his promises, runs away from his problems, and seems to have no compassion for the creature of his own making.

So do we hate Victor? Actually, no. You could say that we understand Victor. We sympathize with his plight in a way that he is never able to do with his monster. You could even say, if you were feeling super gutsy, that Victor is the monster of our own making, of *society's* making. He is born out of our own fears of technology and science. He encapsulates our negative qualities, our shallowness, and our ugliness. Or at least he did in the nineteenth century.

Another gutsy direction you could go is to say that Victor is a self-sacrificing hero, maybe even a Christ figure. What's the rationale? He chooses to give his own life to save mankind from what he believes to be evil in the world. If said evil isn't actually evil so much as loveably ugly, then he's a misguided Christ figure. However, at the same time, he is a most wretched villain, bringing pain to the thing most dear in his life – the product of his own creativity.

Does this sound like about five different, irreconcilable interpretations? Good. That's the point.

Victor Frankenstein Timeline and Summary

- Victor is born in Geneva to parents Alphonse and Caroline Frankenstein.
- His parents adopt Elizabeth with the intention that when the kids are older, they will marry.
- He reads the work of alchemists and forms his view of the world and of science.
- His mother dies of scarlet fever only a few weeks before he is to go away to college. On her deathbed, she again says how much she wants Victor to marry Elizabeth.
- Victor attends the university of Ingolstadt, where he studies chemistry and natural philosophy.
- He becomes a star pupil at the university, learning all his professors can teach him in a few short years.

- After that, he has to take his studies further on his own. It is then that he decides to create the spark of life in an inanimate thing.
- He creates a monster and runs away from it.
- He has a nightmare about Elizabeth and his mother's corpse.
- He runs into Henry Clerval and falls ill.
- Henry nurses him back to health over a period of months.
- They study "Oriental" languages together at Ingolstadt.
- Victor and Henry return home because Victor's brother, William, has been murdered.
- Victor sees the monster in the woods on the way home when he is locked out of the gates of Geneva for the night; he realizes the monster killed William.
- He is too afraid to tell anyone his secret, and partly because of his silence, an innocent, Frankenstein family servant, Justine Moritz, is executed.
- Victor feels remorse and goes off into the mountains. He runs into the monster there.
- The monster asks him to listen to his story, and Victor consents, going to an ice cave with him.
- The monster asks Victor to make him a companion, and Victor reluctantly consents.
- He goes back to Geneva and delays making the companion for the monster.
- His father thinks Victor doesn't want to marry Elizabeth. But he does. Really.
- He says he needs to go on a journey first.
- Henry accompanies him to England, but Victor can't work with him around.
- He sends Henry to stay with his friends in Scotland.
- The monster watches Victor closely, and he sees the monster looking through the window one day while he is working on the she-monster on the desolate island of Orkney.
- Victor realizes what he might release upon humanity if he creates a second monster, so he destroys it and dumps its body parts into the lake that night.
- The winds prevent him from returning to shore.
- He thinks about drowning himself.
- Instead, he sails up to a nearby town, where the people accuse him of murder.
- The magistrate takes him to view the body. It is Henry.
- Victor falls ill for two months.
- He is in jail.
- When he recovers, his father visits him and he gets letters from Elizabeth asking him if he loves another woman.
- The town magistrate takes pity on him. He is acquitted of the charges.
- He rests in Paris and returns to Geneva.
- He is fearful of the monster, who vowed to be with him on his wedding night, but he goes ahead with wedding plans, not realizing the monster's true intent.
- He marries Elizabeth.
- On their wedding night, while Victor is preparing to fight the monster, the monster kills Elizabeth instead of him.
- Victor returns to Geneva. His father dies of grief to hear the news of Elizabeth's death.
- He swears revenge on the monster, and starts out chasing him. He ends up with a dog sled in the Arctic Ocean. Well, not literally *in* the ocean, but pretty close. *On*, perhaps.
- Near death, he boards Captain Walton's ship, and resting, he tells Walton his story.
- He urges the ship not to give up if it ever gets unstuck from the ice.
- He dies.

The monster Character Analysis

The monster comes into the world by a pretty terrible set of circumstances. He has the strength of a giant, yet an infant mind. He has a gentle nature, yet his physical defects hide his goodness and make everyone fear and mistreat him. He is rejected by his own creator because of his hideous looks. His feelings are the most deep and moving of any character's in this novel, as well as the most conflicted.

To make matters more confusing, the monster is compared to both Adam and Satan in *Paradise Lost*. This may seem slightly unclear. The thing to keep in mind is that the idea at the core of the monster is his duality. His very *complex* duality. He is at once man in his pure state before the Fall (the Fall = evil), and yet the incarnation of evil itself (what with all his murdering and such). Hmm…this is starting to sound a little like Victor Frankenstein. Complex duality…conflicting characterization…could it be that the monster resembles his maker in his duality?

Let's talk about his name, and how it *isn't* Frankenstein. This common mistake or mass ignorance is actually illuminating. Since the monster has no name of his own, he's not quite an independent fellow. Instead, he's tied to his creator. He is nothing without Victor. He is as much a part of Frankenstein as he is his own being. So we might as well call him "Frankenstein."

This starts to get at the sob-fest at the end of the text. We, like every other reader, react something like this: "What? We thought Victor and the monster were enemies! What's going on?" Exactly. What *is* going on? The monster may hate Victor, want to take vengeance on him, want to kill all his friends in gruesome and inhuman ways, but that doesn't mean he doesn't love the guy.

Of course, the other reason the monster turns on the water works is that Victor was his last connection to humanity. If you hadn't noticed, the monster is one of many people in this text that suffers from loneliness, solitude, and an all around desire for companionship. Victor may have scorned him, hated him, and tried repeatedly to kill him, but hey, at least he talks to the monster. At least he acknowledges the monster's existence. And for a dude who's spent most of his miserable life in hiding and exile, this can be pretty appealing. Good or bad, Victor is the only relationship he's ever had. The squirrels don't count.

Now, whether or not you'd like to admit it, you teared up a little bit at that ending. Come on, a little bit. Why is that? Because we, the readers, totally like the monster. He's a nice guy. He's compassionate. He's people-smart. He saves a little girl's life. He just gets the shaft because he's ugly. Can we blame him if he lashes out in unexpected and absurdly violent ways?

That's a good question. Do we blame him? Do we hate him? Do we love him? This sounds like more conflicting emotions. Could it be that we, the reader, feel the same duality of emotions that the monster and Victor feel for each other?

OK, so one more thing. What does it mean that the monster is made out of dead-person parts?

If he's made up out of people, then he's basically a person himself. But if they're dead, then he's never really alive in the first place. You could also say that, since he's a hodge-podge of human parts, he's also a potpourri of human qualities. This might explain his duality.

The monster Timeline and Summary

- The monster is created by Victor Frankenstein.
- He tries to connect with people, but even his own creator runs away from him in fear because he is so ugly.
- Victor leaves him alone in his apartment after he wakes up to see the monster smiling at him.
- The monster goes into a house, but the people drive him away.
- He enters a village and a similar thing happens.
- He hides in the hovel outside the house of a group of peasants of whom he grows fond. He lives there through the winter and into the spring.
- He watches them, stealing food from them at first until he realizes they are poor.
- After that, he gathers food in the woods, as well as firewood for the family. He does other chores, too.
- He sees his reflection in water and realizes how ugly he is, and it makes him sad.
- He watches them, learning to speak and read from them.
- He finds books in the woods, including *Paradise Lost*, and reads them, along with journal entries found in the pockets of Victor's clothing.
- He learns of Victor's horror at seeing him and his monstrous nature. He despairs.
- One day, when the young people are gone, he tries to talk to the blind old peasant in hopes of forming some sort of social connection.
- The old man is kind to him, but then the younger people return and drive him away.
- With no more hope in the goodness of humanity, the monster goes off in search of Victor.
- On the way through the woods, he saves a little girl from drowning, but her male companion assumes the monster is attacking her and shoots him in the shoulder.
- He nurses his wound for weeks before making his way to Geneva.
- He sees a boy outside Geneva in the woods who mocks him for being ugly.
- The monster wasn't intending to hurt him, but the boy reveals himself to be William Frankenstein, and the monster, filled with rage at his creator's indifference, kills the boy.
- He plants a picture on Justine to frame her for the murder.
- He sees Victor in the mountains and invites him to a cave to talk by his fire.
- He tells Victor about the peasants and how alone he is, as well as confessing to murdering William out of anger.
- He asks Victor to create him an equally ugly female companion, promising to take her to South America away from the rest of the world.
- Finally, he persuades Victor to make the she-monster.
- He tells Victor that he will know when she is done because he will be monitoring his progress.
- He follows Victor for the two years he travels in England and Scotland while working on the companion.

- He is looking in the window at Victor the night he destroys the companion in second thought.
- He vows to be with Victor on his wedding night and swears revenge.
- The monster kills Henry.
- The monster shows up and kills Elizabeth on the big wedding night.
- He leads Victor around in a final chase lasting for months, leaving clues and trails so that Victor can follow him but never catch him.
- He weeps over Victor's dead body aboard Captain Walton's ship, and tells Captain Walton about himself.
- The monster leaves to build a funeral pyre and die.

Robert Walton Character Analysis

In many ways, Walton's story parallels that of Victor's. He is an exploratory man by nature, on an expedition to the North Pole to make some kind of discovery. Unfortunately, his ship gets stuck in some ice and his men fear they will die. He is torn between discovery and caring for people, much in the same way Victor is. He also writes letters to his sister.

Walton is also lonely in the way Victor and the monster are lonely. He desires a companion above all else, a friend with whom he can talk. He feels that he does not fit into society; he does not have a place, just as the monster does not. His thrill at having Victor arrive on his boat exemplifies his desire for friendship, as does his tragic disappointment when Victor dies.

When his crew asks if they can return to England, he at first says no, but later says yes, after hearing Victor's tale about the overwhelming consequences of pushing the bounds of exploration. He learns from Victor's story, in other words. After Victor dies, he turns the ship back, trying not to make the same mistakes that Victor made in the obsession that ruined his life.

Walton's the only guy that's not a total jerk to the monster. This could just be because he is similarly lonely, or, in the hopeful-Pollyanna sense, it could be that he learned from listening to Victor's tale. Maybe he has some sophisticated and compassionate understanding of the monster, having heard the story? Then again, maybe not.

Robert Walton Timeline and Summary

- Walton is captain of a ship headed for the North Pole.
- He writes his sister a number of letters telling about his travels.
- At first, he thinks the voyage will be successful.
- Soon the ship gets stuck in impassable ice.
- Walton longs for a friend.
- Victor appears and they bring him on board and care for him.

- Walton listens to Victor's stories about his life
- The men on the ship ask to turn around. Victor puts them off for two days, but when they come back, he agrees they should return to England.
- Victor dies.
- Walton sees the monster and talks with him.
- He turns the ship around and heads back to England.

Henry Clerval Character Analysis

Henry is Victor's friend and traveling companion. He attends the university of Ingelstadt with him and nurses him back to health when he falls ill. He travels with Victor on his two-year journey through England and Scotland while he works on the monster's companion. Henry is sent to stay with acquaintances of Victor's in Scotland while he finishes his work. The monster kills him and Victor is accused of being the murderer.

So aside from moving the plot forward, Henry highlights some central themes for us. The first is companionship as opposed to isolation. Victor, Walton, and the monster all end up lonely and in serious need of BFF's. But Victor wasn't always alone. The monster just made sure he ended up that way. By killing Henry, the monster forces Victor to experience the same solitude that he has been stuck with his entire (if short and miserable) life.

Henry is also eye candy. If the monster is the epitome of ugliness, that Henry is his polar opposite, at least in the looks department which, if you've spent any time with Victor Frankenstein, you know is the most important aspect of any person. Yet, and this is the interesting part, Henry's death isn't really that sad. We don't know about you, but we were closer to tears when we saw the monster crying over Victor's body than we were when Henry's bloated corpse was presented to his friend. Good thing we, the reader, have moved past judging books by their covers, even if none of these characters have.

Elizabeth Lavenza Character Analysis

Elizabeth is adopted by Caroline Frankenstein when she is five from a family of poor Italian people. She is beautiful and sweet. She is supposed to marry Victor. When Justine is accused of murder, she believes in her innocence and speaks on her behalf. She writes Victor letters, and worries that he has fallen in love with another woman. But no. Victor marries her, and she is murdered by the monster on her wedding night.

Elizabeth is beautiful, so, based on Victor Frankenstein's logic, she must be a good person. Much as the monster is defined by his ugliness, Elizabeth is defined by her attractiveness. This is most likely why Victor is all happy to marry her. Much like the murder of Henry, the monster kills Elizabeth to drive Victor into isolation. Or possibly to get Victor all to himself.

Alphonse Frankenstein Character Analysis

Victor's father is supportive and kind to Victor. He takes Victor into the mountains when Victor is grieving over Justine's death and his guilt. He travels to visit Victor when he is imprisoned for the death of Henry. When Elizabeth dies, he dies shortly afterwards of grief.

Victor's father is yet another stop on Victor's path to total and complete loneliness. The monster didn't even have to off him; he just went voluntarily. But in all seriousness, Alphonse emphasizes that loneliness really is the worst thing you can suffer. He dies of grief when he loses a family member…and you could easily argue that certain *other* characters (ahem, Victor, ahem, the monster) die for similar reasons: the grief of isolation.

William Frankenstein Character Analysis

William is Victor's younger brother, and the guy who taunts the monster for being ugly when he encounters him in the woods. He tells the monster he is a Frankenstein, and the monster kills him for it.

Oh, William – you're not the brightest crayon in the box. Nor are you the most considerate, the kindest, or the most interesting. You're pretty much the embodiment of all the shallow negativity of the other characters in the story. And, fittingly, you're the monster's first victim.

Justine Moritz Character Analysis

Justine lives with the Frankenstein family as a servant after her mother dies. When William is murdered, the monster puts a photograph that William was carrying in her pocket, and she is accused of murder. She confesses falsely to the crime out of fear of going to Hell. She is executed.

In addition to the people he actually murders, the monster ends up indirectly causing the death of a few others as well. Justine is the first clear example of this. Alphonse is another. This is interesting. If we start blaming the monster for indirectly causing deaths, then we also have to blame Victor for the same crime. Sure – if the monster hadn't killed William, Justine wouldn't have been executed. But, if Victor hadn't created the monster, the monster wouldn't have killed William. See? Once you start down that path, you raise all sorts of questions of blame and morality and responsibility. Which is kind of the point of thinking about *Frankenstein* at all.

Caroline Frankenstein Character Analysis

Caroline is Victor's mother. She adopts Elizabeth in much the same way her husband took her in – to care for her after her father passed away. She cares for Elizabeth when she has scarlet fever and catches it herself, dying when Victor is only seventeen.

Caroline may seem to be a minor character, but she's actually hugely important in explaining Victor's motivations and psyche. Did you notice that Victor gets really into bringing dead things to life after his mother dies? That his obsession with mortality begins with her? Victor is understandably distraught at losing his mother at such a young age; he just chooses to deal with it in a destructive and horrifying manner.

Said destructive and horrifying manner really comes back to bite him on the behind. If Victor brought the monster to life to somehow make up for his mother's death, it is tragically ironic that this act causes the death of the rest of his family.

De Lacey Character Analysis

De Lacey is the Parisian-turned-blind-peasant who lives in the cottage. The monster tries to talk to him. but his children drive him away. De Lacey serves a few different purposes. First, he demonstrates the role of family in juxtaposition to the loneliness that the monster and later Victor feels. He has a son, Felix, and a daughter, Agatha, who both live with him, so he is surrounded by warm fuzzy family feelings all the time. The monster, of course, watches this with envy.

De Lacey being blind is also a huge deal. The monster's claim that "people only hate me because I'm ugly" is essentially validated by this guy. If only everyone were blind, the world would be such a better place.

Felix and Safie Character Analysis

Felix is De Lacey's son. He is sad until Safie comes to live with them, the woman whom he met in a Turkish prison and wants to marry. When he sees the monster, he drives him away.

Hmm, sounds like more about isolation and loneliness. Felix's story is strangely inserted into the center of our story-in-a-story-in-a-story-in-a-story sandwich. We can't even take a bite out of this sucker anymore.

Anyway, there are a lot of complicated theories on just what's going on with the Felix-Safie couple. Lots of feminists use the relationship as an excuse to paint the entire novel in a feminist light. Not that there's anything wrong with that. There's lots of somethings you could say about their relationship. Here's one: Safie ends up with Felix instead of back in Islamic Turkey. In the big-picture sense, she chooses love over societal boundaries. Which is kind of what the monster wants Victor to do – get over the ugliness factor and just be friends, already.

Is this the right interpretation? No, because there isn't one. But give it a shot anyway.

Mr. Kirwin Character Analysis

Mr. Kirwin is the magistrate who accuses Victor of murder, but later is compassionate to him. This guy is mostly an instrument to move the plot forward.

M. Waldman Character Analysis

Waldman is Victor's chemistry professor. He is sympathetic about Victor's interest in alchemy and encourages his study of science. Again, this drives the plot forward.

M. Krempe Character Analysis

Krempe is Victor's natural philosophy professor. He is unsympathetic and even mocking of Victor's interest in alchemy. He encourages Victor to start his studies over. This guy is the worst academic advisor ever.

Character Roles

Protagonist
Victor Frankenstein
We suppose Victor is the primary protagonist, since he is the main person we are concerned with. We see what he wants and we're invested in his character. He also fits the "tragic hero" role as his desires are continually thwarted by forces outside of his control. Well, *sort of* outside his control.

Protagonist
The monster
AND YET, the monster seems more human than any character, including Victor. All the guy wants is compassion and companionship – what's more puppy-dog-protagonist loveable than that? Of all the characters in this story, he is the only one who performs any true acts of grace: he saves the little girl from drowning in the river; he gathers firewood for the peasants at the cottage; he DOESN'T judge people based on their appearances. Indeed, if we read this novel as a creation story, which we sometimes do, the obvious protagonist becomes the monster. He stands in for man confronting the basic human condition of suffering in an indifferent world with an absent God. In this way, we can relate to him far more than to the other characters. They all suffer because they've brought about their own downfall through their own mistakes. (Well, maybe not Elizabeth.) But the monster suffers because he unfairly got the shaft since birth. It's like the epigraph says – did he *ask* for all this? No. Not remotely.

Antagonist
The monster

OK, so the monster didn't ask for all this. But does that really exonerate him? Last we checked, no one was getting off death row with the defense of "I can't be guilty of murder; I didn't *ask* to be born." So when you remember that the guy was in some way responsible for four deaths or so (five if you count Victor), then he stops looking like a sympathetic character. Not to mention, if you went with Victor as the protagonist, the monster, his enemy, is the antagonist by default.

Antagonist
Victor Frankenstein
Well, fine. But, if you went with the monster as a protagonist, then Victor has to be the antagonist (or possibly all of mankind, everywhere. Except for the blind people). Victor antagonizes the monster by refusing to have compassion for him, by refusing to support him after creating him, and by refusing to make him a companion. Lots of refusal going on here. The really sexy analyses claim that both Victor and the monster are antagonists not only to each other, but also to themselves. "Ooooh," you say. Yes, "Ooooh" indeed. And check this out: the namelessness of the monster influences the union of these two characters as both equal parts protagonist and antagonist. In the end, their relationship is the only constant – and they take equal turns destroying it. They bring about their own downfalls through a series of their own poor choices in the imperfect worlds they are presented with. Tragic, isn't it?

Foil
Robert Walton and Victor Frankenstein…and the monster. It's a threesome foil.
Robert is most similar to Victor in his drive to explore the world. He is also similar to the monster in his feelings of utter aloneness and his desire to have some kind of friend. It's almost as if he's the common link between them metaphorically. How appropriate, as he is literally the common link between them at the end of the text.

But Robert isn't exactly like Victor, either. (He's a foil, not just a reflection.) While Victor's explorative tendency leads him to self-destruction and death, Walton chooses to cut short his search for knowledge in favor of life – both his and his crew's. This stands in direct contrast to Victor's ultimate sacrifice of his whole circle of loved ones for the greater good, first of science, and later of humanity. Heavy stuff.

Character Clues

Direct Characterization
Shelley isn't big on the subtle showing. She pretty much tells you what characters are thinking or feeling. With all the complicated symbols and duality and "what does it mean to be human?" questions, we kind of appreciate her tossing us a bone on this one.

Physical Characterization
Well, identifying "looks" as a tool of characterization in *Frankenstein* is kind of like shooting immobile fish in a tiny barrel. While we, the reader, understand that the monster is ugly, it's actually the characters themselves that use looks as a tool of prejudice and unwarranted characterization. Since the monster is ugly, he must be evil. The fun part comes in when the monster actually does become sort of evil, or at least commits evil crimes. He conforms to

everyone's expectations. He becomes the victim of his own characterization.

Literary Devices

Symbols, Imagery, Allegory

Light and Fire

Oh, where to begin. Light is associated with goodness and knowledge. Fire is symbolic of both human progress as well as the dangers of human invention. Er, or possibly the dangers of nature as opposed to humans. You could argue either way.

There's also the whole Prometheus thing. (The alternative title, remember?) Fire was the one thing that man wasn't supposed to have because it belonged solely to the Gods. When Prometheus stole fire for man, it meant that man was trespassing on immortal territory. Which was a big no-no and resulted in Prometheus having his liver eaten out every night for the rest of eternity. OK, so Victor didn't have an organ ripped violently from his lower torso every day. But he *did* suffer a similar form of prolonged torture (think of all his loved ones being singled out and killed). No, he wasn't punished for stealing fire, but he was punished for trespassing on immortal territory by playing God.

All right, now we're rolling. We think the monster quite succinctly summed up the rest when he said something about fire warming you up, but burning you, too. Some things, it seems, bite worse than their bark. Some things (fine, we're thinking the monster and science in general) can be good or evil, depending on how much care you take in approaching them. And in Victor's case, that would be no care at all.

Adam, Eden, Other Biblical Business

The monster is compared to Adam and the creation of man. OK, sure, this would mean Victor is also paralleled with the creator, possibly God, and as some claim, maybe even a Christ-figure given the self-sacrifice of his death. But then Shelley screws with us and compared the monster to the fallen angel, too (that would be Satan). What's the point of confusing the hell out of us? This gets back to that duality business. The complex role of Christian allusions in the text steer the reader away from any one meaning, and remind us that, if we want to wrap up our analysis in a neat little package, we'd better think twice. These allusions establish the duality of both characters; no one is strictly good, and no one is strictly evil. Instead, these characters show a capacity for both good and evil, which, last time we checked, is sort of the human condition.

Exploration

The entire story of exploration for knowledge, as symbolized by Captain Walton's quest for the North Pole, becomes a cautionary tale and allegory about the dangers of boundless science. The entire novel serves in part as a warning against the scientific revolution and its potential for destroying humanity. In contrast to this weird world of "science" (scary stuff) is the sublime world of nature, which is pure and uncorrupted by science.

"But wait," you say, "maybe the book argues *for science.*" Sure. After all, the monster is harmless in nature to begin; it is just Victor's shameless neglect that drives him to murder. Yes, this is an overreaction, but still, the problem isn't science itself; it's the people who abuse it. That sounds like a good counter-argument to us.

Setting

Captain Walton's ship in the North Pole; Europe

Although the frame story is exclusively set aboard Captain Walton's ship in the frozen waters of the Arctic, the events of the story happen all over Europe, from Geneva to the Alps to France, England, and Scotland, as well as the university at Ingolstadt. Since there is a great deal of moving about in this story, and further, since exploration of the unknown (and that includes geography) is one of the over-arching themes, the setting is quite broadly constructed from a whole series of places rather than one singular location. As far as the frame of the story goes, we have some nice contrast between Victor telling his story on icy waters of the ocean and the monster telling his next to a fire in a cave. Think of this as a nice little setting sauce of dual images to compliment your Victor-monster duality chicken.

But what about everyone being stuck in the Arctic? In this text, you might have noticed 1) duality 2) religious references, and 3) mention of lots of old, dead people's books like *Paradise Lost*. You can put this all together in the setting. Being stuck in ice sounds like a pretty hellish experience. We've never experienced it personally, but we can guess. So hellish, in fact, that it sounds particularly reminiscent of Dante's description of the ninth and innermost circle of Hell in *Inferno*. To summarize: The ninth circle of hell is reserved for those who have committed betrayal. All the sinners are *stuck in frozen water*, up to their shoulders or necks or eyes or whatever depending on just how bad their betrayal was. Satan's there, of course, stuck in the middle of the lake and pouting. The worst kind of betrayal, Dante tells us, is betrayal against your God.

If you weren't on the same page as we are, we're thinking the monster betrayed Victor (by killing his family) who is his personal God (because he's his creator). With the book's Christian influences, it's easy to argue that Victor betrayed his own God by trying to play God himself (much like Prometheus betrayed the Gods via his creation – ooh!). And if you want proof that Shelley had Dante in mind, check out paragraph four in chapter five when she describes the monster as that of which "even Dante could not have conceived" (5.4).

You could keep going with this. What does it mean that Walton and his men are freed from the ice? Did Christ-like Victor die for everyone's sins, purging the ship and crew of guilt and freeing them from responsibility? We'll let you do the rest.

Narrator Point of View

First Person (Central Narrators): Robert Walton; Victor Frankenstein; the monster.

This story is told through the frame story of letters written by Walton to his sister. So ultimately, it is all his point of view. But within that frame, Victor tells him his own story. Deeper still, the monster relates to Frankenstein his own experience. So ultimately we have the monster's story as told by Victor as encapsulated by Walton's story. So it is a story within a story within a story.

Genre

Gothic Fiction; Tragedy; Science Fiction

This novel is the first science fiction story – supposedly. It was also quite influenced by the gothic, romantic tradition that incorporates supernatural, horrific events and absurdly exaggerated and dramatized goings-on. Further, everyone ends up dead by the end – pretty much a sure giveaway that the novel is a tragedy.

Tone

Romantic, Gothic, Tragic, Fatalistic

Although there are elements of Romanticism in the text, particularly in regards to descriptions of nature's effects, the story is also Gothic what with all the supernatural and creepy events. Further, the things that happen are sad. People die. That's tragic. The biggest tragedy is that the most human character, the monster, has no outlet for his feelings of benevolence towards humanity. Things also seem to be predestined once a singular act sets them in motion, so that would indicate a certain sense of fatalism here, too.

What's Up With the Title?

Well, Frankenstein is the name of the scientist, Victor Frankenstein, whom the book is about. Congratulations – you now know more than the average Joe, who thinks the monster created by the scientist is named Frankenstein.

"The Modern Prometheus" part refers to this story by Ovid (Greek poet operating roughly around the switch from BC to AD) about a Titan named, surprise, Prometheus. This titan makes man out of clay. As in, the first man (this is a creation story). To make a long Greek tale a shorter and in English, Prometheus crafts the man out of clay, but screws up when he steals fire from the Gods for man to have. He's punished in a ridiculously painful manner. What does this have to do with *Frankenstein*? Well, there is some interesting talk of fire – check out Symbols, Allegory, and Imagery. We noted that Victor Frankenstein decidedly *doesn't* take care of the monster the way Prometheus cared for man. Which could be quite a fine point, depending on how you look at it. It's probably most illuminating to look at the myth in broader sense. Prometheus crafts man. Victor crafts the monster. Prometheus ends up getting his liver eaten out night after night as punishment. Victor ends up having all his family members killed. Both suffer from "playing God," so to speak.

Another way to look at "Modern Prometheus" is to consider that Immanuel Kant actually coined the term in reference to Ben Franklin. Remember his experiments with electricity? Plus, Franklin – Frankenstein – see the similarity? That's about as far as we're going to go for now.

What's Up With the Epigraph?
"Did I request thee, Maker, from my clay
To mould me Man, did I solicit thee
From darkness to promote me?"
– Paradise Lost, X, 743-45

Have you ever screamed at your parents, "Well, I didn't ask to be born!"? Well, that's pretty much how the monster feels about being created by Frankenstein. Also, the clay business gets back to the Prometheus title. Ah, beautiful.

Did You Know?

Trivia

- Mary Shelley claims to have written this story based on a dream she had. She wrote it down for a ghost story contest she was having with friends, but she is the only person who ever finished the writing started for the contest. We're thinking she totally won. (Source)
- Apparently people didn't like Frankenstein – at first. But they got over themselves and Shelley was still around when they did a theatre production in 1823. (Source)
- Shelley at first published anonymously. On January 1st. It was a cheery kick-off to 1818. (Source)

Steaminess Rating

PG
There is nothing to see here, people. Apparently, those in the 18th century did not have sex. Ever. If they even thought about sex, they went around pretending they didn't. Unfortunately for us, they kept it behind closed doors.

Allusions and Cultural References

Literature, Philosophy, and Mythology

- John Milton: _Paradise Lost_ – "Did I request thee, Maker, from my clay/To mould me Man, did I solicit thee/From darkness to promote me?" (Epigraph, 10.9, 15.3)
- Plutarch: _Lives_ (15.3)
- Johann Wolfgang von Goethe: _Sorrows of Werter_
- (15.3)
- Samuel Taylor Coleridge: _Rime of the Ancient Mariner_ (5.8)
- Dante (5.4)
- The myth of Prometheus: (Title, 16.1)
- Constantin-Francois Volney: _Ruins of Empires_ (13.14)

Historical Figures

- Dr. Darwin, not Charles, but his grandfather (The author's preface)
- Cornelius Agrippa (2.6)
- Paracelsus (2.8)
- Albertus Magnus (2.8)

Best of the Web

Movie or TV Productions
Frankenstein Movies
http://www.frankensteinfilms.com/
A comprehensive list of Frankenstein movies.

1994 Movie
http://www.imdb.com/title/tt0109836/
Frankenstein with Robert De Niro as the monster.

1931 Movie
http://www.imdb.com/title/tt0021884/
A old film with the monster taking the classic form that we now associate with the Frankenstein of Halloween costumes.

2004 TV Movie
http://www.imdb.com/title/tt0397430/
A modern take on _Frankenstein_.

Websites

Pop Culture Frankenstein
http://en.wikipedia.org/wiki/Frankenstein_in_popular_culture
This link gives a comprehensive overview of Frankenstein-related things in popular culture.

Made in the USA
Middletown, DE
11 April 2015